A practical guide to

MAGIC
IN
NATURE

A practical guide to

MAGIC IN NATURE

JESSICA LAHOUD

ROCKPOOL

A Rockpool book
PO Box 252
Summer Hill
NSW 2130
Australia

rockpoolpublishing.com
Follow us! **f** ◉ rockpoolpublishing
Tag your images with #rockpoolpublishing

ISBN: 9781922786494

Published in 2025 by Rockpool Publishing
Copyright text © Jessica Lahoud 2025
Copyright design © Rockpool Publishing 2025

All rights reserved. No part of this publication may be reproduced, stored in a retrieval system, or transmitted in any form or by any means, electronic, mechanical, photocopying, recording or otherwise, without the prior written permission of the publisher.

Design and typesetting by Sara Lindberg, Rockpool Publishing
Edited by Heather Millar

 A catalogue record for this book is available from the National Library of Australia

Printed and bound in China
10 9 8 7 6 5 4 3 2 1

For my little
Sun & Moon

CONTENTS

1 Introduction
5 How to use this book

9 Part 1: Crystals
11 Introduction to crystal healing
12 Crystal care
15 How to use crystals
17 How to read the crystal profiles
20 Crystals A–Z

65 Part 2: Plant magic
67 Introduction to plant magic
76 How to read the plant profiles
80 Herbs and spices
98 Flowers and shrubs
120 Fruits and vegetables
138 Roots, resins and woods

151 Part 3: Animals
153 Introduction to animal messengers
156 Animals A–Z

181 Part 4: Celestial bodies
183 Introduction to the planets and stars
184 How to read the celestial body profiles
188 The celestial bodies
189 Our solar system
190 Earth
194 Sun
196 Moon
198 Moon Phases

203 Part 5: The elements
205 Introduction to the elements
206 Working with the elements
206 Earth
207 Wind
208 Water
209 Fire

211 Part 6: The magic in you
213 Introduction to your personal magic
215 Clearing your energy
217 Using tools
220 Chakras
228 Meridians
234 The five elements of TCM
236 Auras

239 Acknowledgements

240 Index

246 About the author

INTRODUCTION

This book is dedicated to those who grew up looking for fairies in their garden, making potions with mud and rocks, playing mermaids at the beach and dreaming of growing up to learn magic. May you always see the magic that surrounds you and the magic within you.

All elements of the natural world exist in a symbiotic relationship, and as such, you will find many cross-references throughout these pages. Explore all that appeals to you. Take what resonates and leave what doesn't. Not everyone will feel the same affinity with crystals as they do for plants, and vice versa. While it's not always possible to substitute items in rituals and spells with those from different categories (like swapping a herb for a candle), it's important to recognise that every individual's magical practice is personal. You may find that these cross-references offer options for substitutions you had not considered, allowing you to introduce a complementary energetic profile to your rituals.

You may wonder why there isn't an entry for every animal, plant, planet and crystal, questioning what the deciding factor is behind this curated list that seems abundant, but perhaps still lacking to some. There are a few points worth mentioning, and I hope this satisfies you as a reader and seeker of knowledge. My goal was to make this book as useful and practical as possible. This meant being discerning about what I included to ensure that the crystals and plants were accessible, the animals recognisable, and the information reliable. Throughout the writing of this book there were many components I chose to omit due to either a lack of information or because an item was very rare and hard to source. The elements chosen were included because of the abundance of information, documentation, history and tradition of their use in rituals and magical practice. Furthermore, it's important to me that when you are given information about working with magic in nature, it is presented in a way that does not intimidate you from

INTRODUCTION ÷ 3

participating, but rather invites you to join in with the natural items that you already have at home or can easily acquire.

If you are looking for a book filled with the rarest gems and endangered or extinct plants, there are other books out there. My hope is that this is the book you reach for when you are formulating your spells, the book that you reference when making sense of a magical experience you've had in nature, and the book you turn to when an animal messenger appears in a dream. I hope this is the book you highlight and fill with notes, bend the corners of your favourite pages on, and truly get a lot of use out of. This book is a reminder of the interconnectedness of all of nature and the inherent magic that flows within and all around you. May it guide you on your spiritual journey, enlighten you with knowledge, and fill you with wonder.

I hope you find the answers you're looking for in these pages.

HOW TO USE THIS BOOK

This is the ultimate reference guide for magical correspondences found in nature. This book is designed to be a go-to resource for understanding and utilising the properties of hundreds of natural items, from herbs and crystals, to woods and more. It is intended to be a guide you can refer back to time and time again. Each section provides details on magical associations and ways to integrate these tools in your practice. Allow this book to be your trusted companion in harnessing the natural energies around you.

Explore cross-references – discover the way that many natural objects, such as herbs and crystals, are interconnected in their magic, and can complement each other when used in magical practice. By combining items with complementary properties, you enhance the magical power of your ritual.

Trust your intuition – this book covers information on a huge variety of natural items. Embrace what feels right for you and your unique practice. Not everything will resonate, and that's okay.

Find substitutions – this reference guide is an amazing resource for finding substitutions to ingredients for your magical workings. If you're in a bind but need to find an ingredient for a specific purpose, refer to these pages and adapt your ritual to the ingredients you have readily available.

INTRODUCTION ÷ 5

A note on using nature elements in your practice

Tread lightly on this big, beautiful, magical earth.

Give more than you take.

Use crystals, animals and plants with reverence.

Have gratitude for the magic and spirits.

Respect cultural traditions and be mindful of not appropriating.

Choose true connection over commercialism.

Be intentional when you are choosing which natural elements to work with.

Remember that nature elements are precious, finite items.

Do no harm.

Be sustainable in your practice.

Trust your intuition: what works for others might not work for you.

Take notes, document, record.

Believe.

PART 1

CRYSTALS

INTRODUCTION TO CRYSTAL HEALING

The use of crystals as magical tools goes back further than the written word. For thousands of years crystals have fascinated and allured humanity, both for their beauty and for their healing properties. While millions of people across the world collect crystals for their decorative qualities or their rarity, crystals hold powerful healing energies that can influence our physical, spiritual and emotional well-being.

In this section, you will learn about how to care for your crystals, ways that you can use crystals for their magical power, and the magical correspondences of over 100 crystals. There is also a list of powerful crystal combinations that can be used to achieve the most commonly requested uses, from protection to psychic power and more. By understanding the magic of crystals and their powerful potential, you're best equipped to integrate and utilise those magical powers in your daily life and as guidance on your spiritual path.

CRYSTAL CARE

Physical care: cleaning your crystals

Many crystals can be unnecessarily damaged if exposed to water, sunlight, oils, excessive handling or salt. These elements are all frequently referred to for energetic cleansing, which is why this note has been included here. Make sure to research individual crystals before deciding which cleaning method is best for your collection. And when in doubt, choose a method that is low risk.

Cleaning with water

Some crystals can be cleaned in water with a scrub brush if they have lots of debris and dirt on them. Others will dissolve or lose their lustre when exposed to water. Generally polished quartzes, agates, chalcedonies and other very hard crystals do well with water exposure. However, it's important to take note of any other minerals present, especially in rough specimens.

If your crystal can tolerate small amounts of water exposure, or if it's on the more fragile side and you're hesitant to immerse it completely, you could also use a soft damp cloth.

Dusting crystals

For easy dusting and reaching small crevices in your crystal clusters, it's best to use a very soft paint brush as a duster, while holding your crystal with a steady hand.

Sun exposure

It is best to keep your crystals out of direct sunlight. When you consider that they have formed under the earth's surface and away from light, it makes sense that sunlight exposure can cause colour changes in some minerals.

Energetic care: cleansing your crystals

Cleansing your crystals accelerates the energetic renewal process, resulting in more efficient and rejuvenated crystals. The energy of crystals can become stagnant after long periods once removed from their natural environment buried deep within the earth. Crystals also retain energy and therefore, after they have been used for a particular ritual, it's best practice to 'reset' the crystal, so to speak. Regular cleansing and mindful care of your crystals is also a great way to build a stronger energetic bond with them, which will make working with them more intimate and effective.

Cleansing with smoke
Allow the smoke from burned herbs to spill over the crystals.

Moonlight
Leave your crystals under the light of the full moon.

Salt

Place your crystals in a bowl of salt overnight.

Ocean

Give your crystals a bath in the ocean or place in a bowl filled with salty ocean water.

Fresh water

Place your crystals in a running stream of fresh water or place in a bowl filled with fresh water.

Visualise

Hold your crystal during meditation and visualise its energy being purified.

Bury

Place the crystal back into the earth overnight.

Sound

Use a crystal singing bowl or tuning fork to surround the crystal with cleansing sounds and frequencies.

Selenite

Place your crystals on a selenite disc or inside a bowl made of selenite overnight.

Flowers or oils

Lavender and frankincense hold high vibrational frequencies. Place a small amount of their oil on your crystals, spray a diluted mist over your crystals, or place your crystals in a bowl filled with fresh lavender flowers and frankincense resin overnight.

A practical guide to **MAGIC IN NATURE**

HOW TO USE CRYSTALS

Some of the ways that you can work with crystals to enjoy their magical properties are listed below.

Keep them close

Wear or carry crystals, whether as jewellery or as small polished stones that you carry in your pocket. By having them within your auric field through the day, you receive constant energetic exposure.

Ceremony

Use in rituals, incorporated into ceremonies or with other natural elements such as plants and animals, to complement and enhance the energy of your ritual.

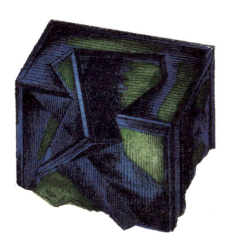

Grids

Make crystal grids in your home or work space, setting an intention for each grid to help you navigate through a particular issue or break through in your spiritual journeying.

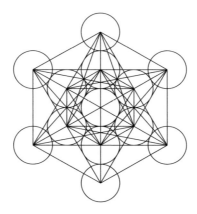

Surround your space

Crystals in your home can enhance the overall energy of your home in all spaces, from the kitchen to the bedroom. You can utilise crystals at the front door to block negative energy from entering, at your bedside to encourage peaceful dreams, in your living room to create a harmonious environment and so on.

Meditate

Crystals can help to promote a meditative state and can be a wonderful addition to your overall meditation experience by enhancing your spiritual connection, potential for healing, and amplification of your intentions.

HOW TO READ THE CRYSTAL PROFILES

In the following section, Crystals A–Z, each crystal is described via the the entries described below.

Name

As the title suggests, this entry is simply the name of the crystal or mineral, followed by any other alternative names it may go by.

Organ/meridian

This entry refers to the corresponding organs of the body in relation to that crystal, according to traditional Daoist crystal healing philosophy. The organs you will see referenced in these entries are as follows: lung, liver, heart, spleen, kidney, stomach, pericardium, gallbladder, triple heater, small intestine, large intestine, bladder.

To learn more about the correspondences of organs and meridians, and how this information can be used in healing, refer to Part 6, page 211.

Chakra

Crystals may resonate with specific energy centres in the body known as chakras. The associated chakra for each crystal is listed to help you further understand the relationship between each crystal, and how they interact with your body on an energetic level. You can also use this as a guide for selecting a collection of crystals for a ritual aimed at a certain energetic need – for

CRYSTALS ÷ 17

example, to make a crystal body grid filled with heart chakra stones to help you cultivate love and compassion for yourself. For a deeper look into chakras, refer to Part 6, page 220.

Mohs hardness

Mohs hardness scale refers to the relative hardness of the crystal: 1 being the softest (talc) going up to 10, which is the hardest (diamond). Knowing the hardness of your mineral can help you decide how to store it to keep it safe and what magical applications are best – for example, very fragile crystals and mineral specimens are best stored in cabinets or boxes, whereas hard crystals that have been tumbled can be carried in your pockets and used in body grids. They can also usually withhold being kept in a communal bowl and don't necessarily require special handling.

Element

Earth, wind, water and fire – these elements make up all of nature. Each element has its own spiritual and metaphysical correspondences. Some crystals are more significantly influenced by a specific element than others. When this happens, the element influences the magical properties of the crystal. For a deeper understanding of the magical correspondences between elements, refer to Part 5, pages 206 to 209.

Properties

Every crystal has unique magical properties that influence your physical, spiritual and emotional bodies. The most prominent properties of each crystal are listed in this section, so you can get a sense of the crystal's energy at a glance.

18 ✦ *A practical guide to* **MAGIC IN NATURE**

CRYSTALS A–Z

Amazonite

Organ/meridian: lung, liver, heart, kidney

Chakra: throat, heart

Mohs hardness: 6–6.5

Element: water

Properties: communication, processing emotions, expressing yourself, calming

Known as a stone of courage, amazonite empowers you to communicate clearly, process your emotions and express yourself authentically.

Amber

Organ/meridian: lung, liver, heart

Chakra: solar plexus

Mohs hardness: 2–2.5

Element: earth

Properties: life force, cleansing, connection to nature, soothing

Harnessing the radiant life force of the sun, amber connects you deeply to the earth's rhythm and brings vitality and renewing energy.

Amethyst

Organ/meridian: lung, liver, heart, spleen, stomach

Chakra: crown, third eye

Mohs hardness: 7

Element: earth, wind

Properties: divinity, sobriety, balance, spirituality, protection

Associated with spiritual awakening, amethyst balances your energy and fosters deep connection to the divine.

Angelite

Organ/meridian: liver, spleen

Chakra: crown, third eye, throat

Mohs hardness: 3–3.5

Element: wind

Properties: communication, connection to angels, tranquillity, meditation

Radiating serene energy, angelite facilitates angelic communication and profound meditative experiences.

Apatite

Organ/meridian: spleen, stomach, kidney

Chakra: third eye

Mohs hardness: 5

Element: wind

Properties: past-life recall, psychic ability, fearlessness, transformation

Opening your mind to past-life experiences, apatite promotes fearless growth and spiritual expansion.

Apophyllite

Organ/meridian: lung, kidney, stomach

Chakra: crown, third eye

Mohs hardness: 4.5–5

Element: wind

Properties: divine light energy, connection to angels, meditation, psychic ability

Radiating divinity, apophyllite acts as a conduit to higher realms and gently supports spiritual journeying.

Aquamarine

Organ/meridian: lung, liver, heart, kidney

Chakra: throat

Mohs hardness: 7.5–8

Element: water

Properties: communication, soothing, releasing anger, trust

Known for cooling down fiery emotions, aquamarine assists with clear communication and promotes peace and harmony.

Aragonite

Organ/meridian: liver, spleen, kidney

Chakra: root, sacral

Mohs hardness: 3.5–4

Element: earth

Properties: grounding, strength, patience, clearing

Grounding and stabilising, aragonite strengthens your connection to the earth and clears away energetic blockages.

Aventurine

Organ/meridian: lung, liver, heart, kidney

Chakra: heart

Mohs hardness: 6.5–7

Element: earth, water

Properties: prosperity, optimism, heart expansion, self-care

Known as the stone of opportunity, aventurine brings luck and abundance into your life while encouraging compassion and love.

Azurite

Organ/meridian: liver, heart, kidney

Chakra: crown, third eye

Mohs hardness: 3.5–4

Element: wind

Properties: focus, intuition, psychic ability, fearlessness

While facilitating profound spiritual growth, azurite enhances mental clarity and psychic expansion.

BLACK TOURMALINE

Organ/meridian: lung, kidney

Chakra: root

Mohs hardness: 7–7.5

Element: earth

Properties: protection, shielding, vacuums negative vibrational frequencies, grounding

Known for its protective qualities, black tourmaline shields against psychic attacks and low vibrational frequencies that cause discord in your life, and its grounding properties promote harmony and stability.

BLOODSTONE

> Organ/meridian: lung, liver, heart, stomach, small intestine, large intestine
>
> Chakra: root
>
> Mohs hardness: 7
>
> Element: earth
>
> Properties: courage, resilience, health, setting boundaries, detoxification

Known for enhancing health and vitality, bloodstone empowers you to create healthy habits both emotionally and physically.

Blue calcite
Organ/meridian: liver, kidney
Chakra: third eye, throat
Mohs hardness: 3
Element: water
Properties: tranquillity, emotional processing, release, expression, intuition

Emanating tranquil energy, blue calcite assists with releasing emotions, habits and energies that hold you back, facilitating space for self-expression and peace in your life.

Blue lace agate
Organ/meridian: lung, liver, spleen, kidney
Chakra: throat
Mohs hardness: 6.5–7
Element: water
Properties: serenity, communication, emotional stability, acceptance

Known as the stone of angelic communication, blue lace agate's calming energy is serene, encouraging gentle communication, understanding and inner peace.

Blue tourmaline (indicolite)
Organ/meridian: lung, liver, kidney
Chakra: third eye
Mohs hardness: 7–7.5
Element: wind, water
Properties: psychic expansion, clairvoyance, expression

A conduit for spiritual expansion, blue tourmaline enhances your psychic gifts and empowers you to express yourself with clarity and conviction.

Calcite
Organ/meridian: lung, liver, heart, stomach, kidney
Chakra: third eye, crown
Mohs hardness: 3
Element: wind, fire
Properties: harmony, balance, serenity, awakening

With its harmonising energy, calcite promotes overall well-being and guides you forward on a path of spiritual alignment.

Carnelian

Organ/meridian: lung, liver, heart, spleen, kidney, stomach

Chakra: sacral, root

Mohs hardness: 7

Element: fire

Properties: creativity, overcoming fears, confidence, action

A stone of courage and vitality, carnelian emboldens you to step into your power to create your own destiny and boosts your motivation and determination.

Cavansite

Organ/meridian: liver, heart, spleen, kidney

Chakra: crown, third eye

Mohs hardness: 3–4

Element: wind

Properties: truth, expression, intuition, determination

Known for its ability to enhance spiritual connection, cavansite facilitates deep meditative states and allows for increased intuition, clarity and communication, empowering you to speak your truth and pursue your dreams.

Celestite (celestine)

Organ/meridian: liver, kidney, stomach

Chakra: crown, third eye

Mohs hardness: 3–3.5

Element: wind

Properties: connection to angels, comforting energy, speaking up, peace

Known for emanating supportive and nurturing energies, celestite connects you to divine angelic realms and inspires you to speak your truth with grace and compassion.

Chalcedony

Organ/meridian: lung, spleen, kidney

Chakra: third eye, heart

Mohs hardness: 7

Element: wind, water

Properties: calming, communication, balance, comfort

Fostering emotional balance and promoting goodwill, chalcedony envelops you in a blanket of harmony that leaves you feeling safe to express yourself.

Charoite

Organ/meridian: kidney, liver, pericardium

Chakra: crown, third eye, solar plexus

Mohs hardness: 5–6

Element: wind

Properties: transformation, spiritual growth, protection, intuition

A stone of transformation and protection, charoite guides you on a journey of spiritual evolution and deepened intuition while shielding you from negative energies and external influences.

Chiastolite

Organ/meridian: liver, heart, spleen, stomach

Chakra: sacral

Mohs hardness: 5–5.5

Element: earth, fire

Properties: grounding, protection, past-life recall

Known for transmuting low vibrational energies into higher, more usable energies, chiastolite offers guardianship and protection while facilitating past-life recollection.

Chrysocolla

Organ/meridian: lung, liver, kidney

Chakra: throat, heart

Mohs hardness: 2–4

Element: water

Properties: self-awareness, expression of truth, creativity, wisdom

Known for awakening inner truth, trust and awareness, chrysocolla encourages you to express yourself fearlessly and to unearth your hidden creativity and talents.

CRYSTALS ÷ 27

Chrysoprase

Organ/meridian: liver, heart, gallbladder

Chakra: heart, solar plexus

Mohs hardness: 7

Element: water

Properties: happiness, joy, manifesting, creativity, abundance

Assisting as you journey into prosperity and elevating your spirits, chrysoprase is known for inviting wealth and blessings into your life while encouraging joy as you welcome these opportunities.

Cinnabar

Organ/meridian: lung, heart, triple heater

Chakra: sacral, root

Mohs hardness: 2–2.5

Element: fire

Properties: transformation, pleasure, wealth, confidence

A highly empowering crystal, cinnabar instils a strong sense of self-worth and drive, enhancing your potential for manifesting success and encouraging transformation and personal growth.

INTERESTING FACT: cinnabar contains the heavy metal mercury. Cinnabar crystals should not be heated, ground into a powder or eaten. It is perfectly safe to handle or wear in jewellery, with consideration – for example, it is not recommended to wear cinnabar for months on end due to the ongoing exposure to mercury, but a few days here and there shouldn't be a problem.

CITRINE

Organ/meridian: lung, spleen, kidney, stomach
Chakra: solar plexus, sacral, root
Mohs hardness: 7
Element: fire
Properties: abundance, happiness, empowerment, optimism

Radiating the abundant energy of the sun, citrine invites joy and prosperity into your life while amplifying your confidence. One of the most powerful manifestation crystals available due to its vibrant energy and motivation-enhancing qualities, citrine's high vibrational frequency is so powerful that it helps to dispel negative energy.

INTERESTING FACT: the majority of citrine sold today is actually heat treated, or radiation-exposed amethyst. Natural citrine is quite rare. It was once thought to be a lot more common, so as the demand became far greater than the supply, suppliers began heating pale amethyst to produce the bright yellow quartz crystals that we now see marketed as citrine.

Clear quartz

Organ/meridian: lung, liver, spleen, kidney, stomach

Chakra: crown, third eye, throat, heart, solar plexus, sacral, root

Mohs hardness: 7

Element: earth, wind, water, fire

Properties: decision making, clarity, amplifies other crystals, transmutes energy

Often referred to as the master crystal, clear quartz is as versatile as it is abundant. Quartz amplifies the energy of other crystals, spells, emotions and so on. Its amplifying qualities make it invaluable as it can be utilised in meditation to boost any focused intention, making it an alternative for almost any other crystal. Useful in meditation, study and work, clear quartz promotes mental clarity and focus.

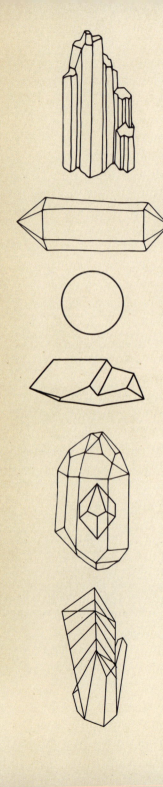

MEANINGS OF QUARTZ CRYSTAL SHAPES

Twin flame
When two crystals form side by side. Used for manifesting a soulmate.

Double termination
A quartz crystal with a terminated point at both the top and bottom of the crystal. Focuses energy in both directions.

Sphere
Manufactured into the shape of a crystal ball. Sphere shapes emanate energy in all directions, amplify and are used for scrying.

Faden quartz
A flattened, self-healed crystal that can enhance the connection between a healer and their client, or encourage healing in an individual.

Manifestation quartz
A small crystal point that has formed within another larger quartz crystal. Used to bring guidance towards achieving your dreams.

Phantom
A crystal with visible layers of growth formation, appearing like many crystals within one crystal. Symbolic of the many phases of our growth, phantom crystals assist us in integrating and navigating through the many layers and challenges towards our emotional healing.

Cuprite

Organ/meridian: liver

Chakra: sacral, root

Mohs hardness: 3.5–4

Element: earth

Properties: grounding, strength, endurance, life-force energy

Cuprite enhances your vitality and stabilises your energy, connecting you to the earth's natural rhythm. It encourages resilience and personal power to overcome challenges.

Dalmatian jasper

Organ/meridian: kidney

Chakra: root

Mohs hardness: 5–7.5

Element: earth

Properties: grounding, gentle protection, playfulness, harmony

Bringing a sense of joy and playfulness into your life, dalmatian jasper's protective and grounding energy offers balance and harmony.

Danburite

Organ/meridian: lung, liver

Chakra: crown, heart

Mohs hardness: 7–7.5

Element: wind

Properties: spirit communication, calming, sleep aid, expansion of consciousness

Known for its high vibration, danburite aids spiritual enlightenment, divine connection and meditation, as well as promoting peaceful, calming energy that helps with sleep and stress.

Desert rose

Organ/meridian: lung, stomach

Chakra: crown, root

Mohs hardness: 2

Element: earth, wind

Properties: higher self-guidance, clarity, meditation, aura cleansing

An ally for times that require sharp focus and mental clarity, desert rose has a gentle energy that is purifying and emotionally supportive.

Diamond

Organ/meridian: liver, kidney

Chakra: crown, third eye, throat, heart, solar plexus, sacral, root

Mohs hardness: 10

Element: earth, wind, water, fire

Properties: purity, amplification, spiritual connection

A powerful amplifying stone, diamond enhances energy,

thoughts and intentions, as well as promoting mental clarity and manifesting power while shielding from negativity.

Diopside

Organ/meridian: lung, liver, gallbladder, triple heater

Chakra: heart

Mohs hardness: 5.5–6

Element: earth

Properties: release, emotional healing, transformation, forgiveness

Diopside promotes emotional well-being and healing, encouraging personal growth and understanding while aiding you in processing and releasing the mental and emotional burdens that stifle you.

Dioptase

Organ/meridian: lung, liver, spleen, gallbladder

Chakra: heart, solar plexus

Mohs hardness: 5

Element: water

Properties: manifesting, compassion, expansion, spirituality

While promoting heart healing and spiritual expansion, dioptase has a vibrant energy that encourages compassion, openness and a willingness to receive.

Dragon's blood jasper

Chakra: heart, root

Mohs hardness: 7

Element: fire

Properties: strength, courage, protection. grounding

Dragon's blood jasper instils courage and strength, empowering you to overcome obstacles while grounding and protecting you.

Dumortierite

Organ/meridian: liver, spleen, stomach

Chakra: third eye

Mohs hardness: 7

Element: wind

Properties: divine guidance, mental focus, perseverance, intuition

Dumortierite inspires resilience and persistence in achieving your goals, helping to alleviate stress and enhance concentration while promoting a strong divine connection.

EMERALD

Organ/meridian: liver, heart, gallbladder

Chakra: heart

Mohs hardness: 7.5–8

Element: water

Properties: love, prosperity, abundance, compassion

Known for its ability to attract love and abundance, emerald promotes harmony in your relationships and encourages heart expansion.

Epidote

Organ/meridian: liver, spleen, kidney, gallbladder

Chakra: heart

Mohs hardness: 6–7

Element: earth

Properties: growth, abundance, manifesting, amplification

Epidote amplifies your intentions to make way for the realisation of your manifested desires, and promotes a positive mindset that leads to personal growth and gratitude.

Fire agate

Organ/meridian: triple heater

Chakra: solar plexus, sacral, root

Mohs hardness: 6–7

Element: fire

Properties: passion, creativity, grounding, vitality

Known for its fiery energy that stimulates motivation and determination for success, fire agate inspires creativity while stifling fears and hesitations.

Fluorite

Organ/meridian: lung, liver, heart

Chakra: third eye, heart

Mohs hardness: 4

Element: water

Properties: cleansing, stress relief, focus, decision making

Fluorite encourages decisive thinking and stabilises your energy while enhancing mental clarity and focus, making it the ideal stone for students, learning and teaching.

Fuchsite

Organ/meridian: liver, kidney

Chakra: heart

Mohs hardness: 3

Element: water

Properties: heart healing, self-love, connection to nature, abundance

Promoting connection to nature, health and abundance, fuchsite assists in processing emotional distress and encourages self-love.

Fulgurite

Chakra: crown, third eye, throat, heart, solar plexus, sacral, root

Mohs hardness: 6.5

Element: earth, wind, water, fire

Properties: amplification, divine connection, manifesting, transformation

Formed by the powerful collision of lightning and earth, fulgurite solidifies the union between earthly connection and divine inspiration.

CRYSTALS ÷ 35

It is useful in manifesting, psychic expansion and transformation.

Garnet

Organ/meridian: lung, heart, kidney

Chakra: root

Mohs hardness: 6.5–7.5

Element: earth

Properties: emotional strength, grounding, sense of security, manifesting goals

Garnet is a stone of ambition and stability, promoting courage and strength to overcome challenges and manifest dreams.

Goethite

Organ/meridian: liver, spleen

Chakra: root

Mohs hardness: 5–5.5

Element: earth

Properties: grounding, transformation, earth connection, manifesting

Goethite facilitates the grounding and releasing of negative energy and emotional burdens, enhancing your manifesting power while keeping you rooted in the earth's stabilising energy.

Green calcite

Organ/meridian: liver, heart

Chakra: heart

Mohs hardness: 3

Element: earth

Properties: heart expansion, renewal, relaxation, positivity

Known for promoting renewed energy, positivity and relaxation while encouraging compassion, forgiveness and stress, green calcite is a beacon of hope during times of change or trouble.

Green tourmaline

Organ/meridian: liver, heart, kidney

Chakra: heart

Mohs hardness: 7–7.5

Element: water

Properties: vitality, manifesting, heart healing, emotional healing

Encouraging an open heart and emotional healing, green tourmaline enhances the energy in your creative centre and strengthens your power of abundance and prosperity.

Hematite

Organ/meridian: liver, pericardium

Chakra: root

Mohs hardness: 5.5–6.5

Element: earth
Properties: grounding, stability, strength, protection

Providing grounding and protection while helping to transmute low vibrational energy, hematite offers stability in both the emotional and energetic sense.

Hemimorphite
Organ/meridian: liver
Chakra: third eye, throat, heart
Mohs hardness: 4.5–5
Element: wind, water
Properties: joy, communication, emotional healing, spirituality

Hemimorphite is a crystal of happiness and expression, encouraging open communication while aiding in spiritual growth and psychic expansion.

Howlite
Organ/meridian: liver, heart, spleen
Chakra: crown
Mohs hardness: 3.5
Element: wind
Properties: calming, dissipates anger, stillness, sleep improvement

Known for its calming energy, howlite reduces stress and anger, assists with sleep issues and encourages deep meditative states.

Indigo gabbro (mystic merlinite)
Chakra: third eye, root
Mohs hardness: 6
Element: earth
Properties: centring, expansion, intuition, transformation

Indigo gabbro has a stable, centred energy that facilitates deep physical, emotional and energetic healing. It promotes psychic expansion and allows you to connect to higher realms, enhancing intuition and promoting spiritual transformation.

Iolite
Organ/meridian: kidney, triple heater, bladder
Chakra: third eye
Mohs hardness: 7–7.5
Element: wind
Properties: visions, intuition, introspection, psychic power

Iolite opens your psychic channels to allow higher consciousness and transcendent experiences while promoting inner vision, deep introspection and understanding.

Jade

Organ/meridian: kidney

Chakra: heart

Mohs hardness: 6–7

Element: earth

Properties: health, well-being, harmony, life-force energy

Revered for its health benefits, jade promotes physical and emotional well-being and strength. It strengthens life-force energy while attracting good fortune and prosperity.

Kunzite

Organ/meridian: liver, heart, spleen

Chakra: heart

Mohs hardness: 6.5–7

Element: water

Properties: release, heart alignment, compassion, love

Kunzite encourages an open heart, compassion, love and emotional healing, allowing you to release anything that is preventing free-flowing love, whether on the giving or receiving end. It teaches you that you are always worthy and deserving of love.

Kyanite

Organ/meridian: liver, kidney

Chakra: crown, third eye, throat, heart, solar plexus, sacral, root

Mohs hardness: 4.5–7

Element: wind, water

Properties: intuition, clears blockages, expression, lucid dreaming

Blue kyanite is known for its ability to break through energetic blockages in your body, balancing your energetic centres and enhancing your potential for psychic experiences.

Labradorite

Organ/meridian: liver, kidney, gallbladder

Chakra: crown, third eye, throat, heart, solar plexus, sacral, root

Mohs hardness: 6–6.5

Element: wind

Properties: transformation, protection, intuition, past-life recall

Known as the stone of magic, labradorite enhances your innate magical powers and promotes transformative growth. It protects against energy vampires and psychic attack.

LAPIS LAZULI

Organ/meridian: liver, heart, kidney
Chakra: third eye, throat
Mohs hardness: 5–5.5
Element: wind
Properties: prophecy, expression, inner truth, protection

Lapis encourages the exploration of personal truth while facilitating the expression of it. It stimulates the third-eye chakra, enhancing spiritual journeying and connection to the divine.

Larimar
Organ/meridian: liver, gallbladder
Chakra: throat
Mohs hardness: 4.5–5
Element: water
Properties: communication, serenity, sleep, emotional healing

Known for its soothing energy, larimar promotes sleep and relaxation while helping to soothe emotional turmoil. It enhances self-expression and encourages you to connect with nature.

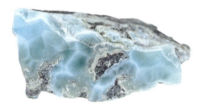

Lepidolite
Organ/meridian: liver, heart, pericardium, gallbladder
Chakra: third eye, heart
Mohs hardness: 2.5–3
Element: water
Properties: stress relief, acceptance, harmony, wisdom

One of the most useful crystals during emotional upheaval, anxiety or overwhelm, lepidolite promotes calm and balance, reduces stress and supports you during challenging circumstances.

Libyan desert glass (golden tektite, Egyptian glass)
Chakra: crown, third eye, throat, heart, solar plexus, sacral, root
Mohs hardness: 5–6
Element: fire
Properties: abundance, prosperity, manifesting, creative expansion, joy

A high vibrational glass formed by an ancient meteoric impact, Libyan desert glass aids in spiritual transformation and awakening. It enhances manifesting power and increases willpower and motivation, and its vibrant energy has the power to boost your mood and encourage a positive mindset.

Lodestone (magnetite)
Organ/meridian: liver, heart, kidney
Chakra: crown, third eye, throat, heart, solar plexus, sacral, root
Mohs hardness: 5.5–6.5
Element: earth
Properties: finding true purpose, attracting life path, healing, grounding

Known for its powerful magnetic qualities, lodestone is a master attractor, aligning you with your life path to fulfilment. Its grounding properties promote harmonious energy flow.

Malachite

Organ/meridian: liver, spleen, stomach

Chakra: heart, solar plexus

Mohs hardness: 3.5–4

Element: fire

Properties: strength, heart healing, finding your life path, perseverance

Malachite is a powerful heart healer encouraging resilience and growth. Its energy shifts heavy emotions rapidly, giving you the strength to push through challenges.

Meteorite

Organ/meridian: liver, heart, kidney

Chakra: crown, third eye, throat, heart, solar plexus, sacral, root

Mohs hardness: 4–7

Element: earth, wind, water, fire

Properties: grounded spiritual expansion, divine connection, vitality, physical healing

Stony meteorite promotes spiritual awakening while facilitating deep connection to the divine. Iron meteorite provides strength and resilience, grounding spiritual energies into your physical reality.

Moldavite

Organ/meridian: liver, heart, kidney

Chakra: crown, third eye, throat, heart, solar plexus, sacral, root

Mohs hardness: 5.5–7

Element: earth, wind, water, fire

Properties: cosmic expansion, transformation, rebirth, unity

Moldavite is a stone of transformative awakening, accelerating your personal and spiritual growth. It enhances your psychic gifts and opens opportunities for you to align your life with your highest purpose.

Mookaite

Organ/meridian: liver, heart, spleen, stomach

Chakra: solar plexus, sacral, root

Mohs hardness: 7

Element: earth

Properties: ancestral guidance, grounding, karmic cycles, earth medicine

Mookaite promotes strength, stability and connection to the earth. It facilitates healing on an ancestral and karmic level, allowing you to be led by your guides and ancestors towards a path of redemption.

Moonstone

Organ/meridian: lung, liver, kidney

Chakra: crown, third eye

Mohs hardness: 6–6.5

Element: wind

Properties: beginnings, self-care, psychic shield, goddess energy

Moonstone assists as you navigate the many phases of your life, offering support during times of transition. Its calming energy promotes gentleness and self-care while alleviating stress and anxieties.

Morganite

Organ/meridian: lung, heart, kidney

Chakra: heart

Mohs hardness: 7.5–8

Element: water

Properties: divine feminine, comfort, self-love, relationship healing

Morganite attracts love and peace, encourages self-love and enhances your capacity for flowing energy in your heart centre. It facilitates stronger relationship bonds, allowing for deep joy and meaningful connection.

OBSIDIAN

Organ/meridian: lung, heart, kidney

Chakra: root

Mohs hardness: 5.5

Element: earth

Properties: protection, shadow work, clarity, grounding

Black obsidian is a powerful protection stone that offers grounding and cleansing properties. It can be used as a scrying mirror, revealing hidden information, or as a deflector, repelling unwanted energies or psychic attacks.

INTERESTING FACT: *most obsidian carvings sold today are manufactured glass. Naturally formed obsidian is increasingly difficult to source. The sudden increase in mainstream crystal popularity has meant the demand for natural obsidian is higher than the availability.*

It's important to note that coloured glasses are also misleadingly sold as natural obsidian – a common example is 'blue obsidian', which is synthetic. While naturally formed obsidian is a glass, it is not ethical to refer to all glass as obsidian.

Ocean jasper

Organ/meridian: heart, pericardium, triple heater, small intestine

Chakra: throat, heart, solar plexus

Mohs hardness: 7

Element: earth

Properties: emotional growth, hope, empowerment, compassion

Ocean jasper encourages introspection and healing, facilitating a shift in perspective to allow for growth. It empowers while instilling hope, allowing you to release stress and negativity.

Opal

Organ/meridian: liver, heart, spleen, kidney

Chakra: crown, third eye, throat, heart, solar plexus, sacral, root

Mohs hardness: 5.5–6.5

Element: earth, wind, water, fire

Properties: joy, abundance, endless potential, wonder

Opal enhances manifesting power and fills your life with majesty and joy. It encourages unique expression and freedom while enhancing creativity and imagination.

Orange calcite

Organ/meridian: liver, heart, spleen, stomach

Chakra: solar plexus, sacral

Mohs hardness: 3

Element: fire

Properties: empowerment, leadership, willpower, courage

Orange calcite encourages creativity and inspiration. It strips away fear, empowers you to take risks and offers the courage required to chase your dreams.

PEARL

> Organ/meridian: liver, heart, kidney
> Chakra: crown, heart
> Mohs hardness: 2.5
> Element: water
> Properties: purity, sensitivity, peace, love, serenity

Unlike most gemstones, pearl is formed in the sea. Emanating purity and wisdom, emotional balance and calmness, it imbues you with a gentle energy that promotes harmony and love.

PERIDOT

> Organ/meridian: liver, heart, spleen, bladder
> Chakra: heart, solar plexus
> Mohs hardness: 6.5–7
> Element: earth
> Properties: heart expansion, happiness, stress relief, opportunity

Peridot is a crystal of abundance and joy that facilitates opportunities and attracts wealth. It encourages a positive mindset and a willingness to open up to others.

Pink tourmaline

Organ/meridian: liver, heart, kidney

Chakra: heart

Mohs hardness: 7–7.5

Element: water

Properties: love, calming, stress relief, emotional healing

Known for its powerful heart-healing properties, pink tourmaline encourages you to process your emotions and make space for love. Its gentle nurturing qualities alleviate anxieties and encourage comfort and security.

Prehnite

Organ/meridian: liver, spleen, kidney, stomach

Chakra: heart, solar plexus

Mohs hardness: 6–6.5

Element: earth, water

Properties: emotional awareness, gentleness, connection to nature, self-worth

Prehnite enhances your inner knowing, sense of self and self-worth. It promotes deep inner connection with yourself, with your guides, and with the natural world around you.

Pyrite

Organ/meridian: liver, stomach

Chakra: solar plexus

Mohs hardness: 6–6.5

Element: earth

Properties: ambition, manifesting will, strength, vitality

Pyrite is a grounding stone that helps to draw your creative and manifesting power down into your physical reality while encouraging perseverance and positivity.

Rainbow obsidian

Organ/meridian: liver, stomach

Chakra: heart, root

Mohs hardness: 5.5

Element: earth

Properties: purification, hope, self-acceptance, self-love, protection

Rainbow obsidian encourages a positive mindset and hope. It assists in the releasing of energies that prevent personal growth while enhancing self-love and acceptance.

Red aventurine

Organ/meridian: lung, liver, heart, kidney

Chakra: sacral, root

Mohs hardness: 6.5–7

Element: earth, fire

Properties: removes fear, grounding, stability, passion

Red aventurine eliminates fears and anxieties that prevent you from progressing towards your goals while encouraging action and passion.

Red jasper

Organ/meridian: heart, pericardium, triple heater, small intestine

Chakra: sacral, root

Mohs hardness: 6.5–7

Element: earth

Properties: courage, improved memory, creativity, determination

Known for promoting emotional strength and endurance, red jasper balances your energy to bring focus and stability into your life.

Rhodochrosite

Organ/meridian: liver, heart

Chakra: heart, solar plexus

Mohs hardness: 3.5–4

Element: fire

Properties: compassion, self-love, calming, relief

Rhodochrosite encourages empathy and understanding. It centres your energy into your heart space to allow free-flowing love for others and yourself.

Rhodonite

Organ/meridian: lung, heart, kidney

Chakra: heart, root

Mohs hardness: 5.5–6

Element: fire

Properties: open heart, love, kindness, determination

Rhodonite is a powerful heart healer that balances emotions and promotes nurturing energy, kindness and love.

Rose quartz

Organ/meridian: heart, liver, stomach

Chakra: heart

Mohs hardness: 7

Element: wind

Properties: universal love, nurturing, forgiveness, compassion

Known as the stone of love, rose quartz enhances your capacity for compassion and harmony in relationships while encouraging an openness for intimacy in your life.

Ruby

Organ/meridian: liver, heart, kidney

Chakra: heart, root

Mohs hardness: 9

Element: earth

Properties: courage, confidence, self-love, passion

Ruby energises and balances your heart centre. It promotes passion and enthusiasm while offering courage to follow your dreams.

Ruby fuchsite

Organ/meridian: liver, heart, kidney

Chakra: heart, root

Mohs hardness: 3–9

Element: water

Properties: self-love, deep introspection, empowerment, forgiveness

Ruby fuchsite is the combination of two powerful heart stones, both of which facilitate deeper loving connection, empathy, compassion and emotional growth.

Rutile

Organ/meridian: lung, liver, spleen, kidney, stomach

Chakra: crown, third eye, throat, heart, solar plexus, sacral, root

Mohs hardness: 7

Element: earth, wind, water, fire

Properties: rapid manifestation, energy amplification, transformation, intuitive expansion

Known for its manifesting qualities, rutile enhances the energy in your creative centre, boosting your potential for transformation and change.

Sapphire

Organ/meridian: liver, heart, stomach

Chakra: third eye, throat

Mohs hardness: 9

Element: wind

Properties: intuition, imagination, expression of self, leadership

Sapphire enhances your wisdom, intuitive awareness and mental clarity. It promotes inner peace, calming energies and spiritual growth.

SELENITE

Organ/meridian: lung, stomach, bladder

Chakra: crown

Mohs hardness: 2

Element: wind

Properties: purifying, tranquillity, divine light energy, clears energetic blockages

Selenite purifies the energies of people, places and things. It is useful for cleansing other crystals, in cord-cutting rituals and for introducing divine white light energy.

Septarian

Organ/meridian: lung, liver, kidney, stomach

Chakra: root

Mohs hardness: 3.5–4

Element: fire

Properties: earth connection, stability, balance, willpower

Septarian nurtures and balances, providing stability. It enhances your connection to nature while promoting confidence and determination.

Seraphinite

Organ/meridian: lung, liver, heart, spleen

Chakra: crown, third eye, throat, heart, solar plexus, sacral, root

Mohs hardness: 2.5–4

Element: earth, wind, water, fire

Properties: psychic enhancement, spiritual evolution, angelic communication, vitality

Seraphinite is known for its powerful connection to the angelic realm. It enhances healing on all levels and brings peace to your mind, body and spirit.

Serpentine

Organ/meridian: lung, liver, stomach, spleen

Chakra: heart, root

Mohs hardness: 3–6

Element: earth

Properties: peace, ancient knowledge, transformation, abundance, connection to earth

Serpentine awakens the ancient knowledge stored inside you, promoting spiritual growth and enlightenment. It facilitates a deep connection to nature and self.

Shungite

Organ/meridian: kidney, bladder

Chakra: crown, third eye, throat, heart, solar plexus, sacral, root

Mohs hardness: 3.5–4

Element: earth, wind, water, fire

Properties: electromagnetic protection, harmony, purification, grounding

Shungite has a gentle nurturing energy that comforts and supports while purifying heavy and stagnant energies and habits. Place it in your bedroom to protect you from electric and magnetic fields (EMFs) while you sleep and promote physical healing.

CRYSTALS ÷ 51

SMOKY QUARTZ

> Organ/meridian: liver, spleen, kidney, stomach
> Chakra: root
> Mohs hardness: 7
> Element: earth
> Properties: grounding, stress relief, clarity, cleansing

Smoky quartz is a powerfully grounding crystal that dissipates negative energy to alleviate stress and anxiety. It aids in focus and clarity, which in turn assists in productivity and overcoming challenges.

Snowflake obsidian

Organ/meridian: lung, liver, heart, kidney

Chakra: third eye, root

Mohs hardness: 5–5.5

Element: earth

Properties: protection, balance, grounding, release

Snowflake obsidian helps to balance your mind and body by releasing negativity and promoting personal growth. These protective qualities promote transformation.

Sodalite

Organ/meridian: lung, liver, kidney, stomach

Chakra: third eye

Mohs hardness: 5.5–6

Element: wind

Properties: intuition, mental focus, wisdom, spiritual expansion

Known for its ability to sharpen your focus and clear your mind, sodalite offers enhanced intuition and wisdom. It promotes understanding, psychic power and deep spiritual insight.

Staurolite

Organ/meridian: liver, spleen, stomach

Chakra: crown, third eye, root

Mohs hardness: 7–7.5

Element: earth

Properties: grounding, divine connection, manifesting, harmony

Known as the fairy stone, staurolite connects you to the fae realm and to the divine. It brings good luck while promoting peace.

Sugilite

Organ/meridian: liver, heart, kidney

Chakra: crown, third eye

Mohs hardness: 5.5–6.5

Element: wind

Properties: purification, protection, psychic power, transformation

A stone of purification and power, sugilite dispels unwanted energies and spirits while enhancing your intuition.

Sunstone

Organ/meridian: heart, kidney

Chakra: solar plexus, sacral

Mohs hardness: 6–6.5

Element: fire

Properties: release, heart alignment, compassion, love

Sunstone is an energising stone that fills you with joy and purpose. It encourages positivity and self-empowerment.

Tanzanite

Organ/meridian: spleen, gallbladder, bladder

Chakra: crown, third eye, throat

Mohs hardness: 6–7

Element: wind

Properties: psychic power, intuition, spirituality, communication

Tanzanite enhances your clairvoyant gifts, expanding your psychic awareness and connecting you to a greater power. It fosters a deep sense of calm and peace, making it useful in meditation.

Tiger eye

Organ/meridian: liver, spleen, stomach

Chakra: solar plexus, sacral, root

Mohs hardness: 6.5–7

Element: earth, fire

Properties: courage, determination, confidence, willpower

Tiger eye enhances your endurance, persistence and motivation. It enables you to overcome obstacles and dig deep for inner strength during difficult times.

TURQUOISE

Organ/meridian: lung, liver, stomach, kidney

Chakra: throat

Mohs hardness: 5-6

Element: earth, wind, water, fire

Properties: expression, grounding, protection, balance

A stone of healing and guidance, turquoise offers protection from discordant energies by keeping you grounded and connected to the earth.

UNAKITE

Organ/meridian: heart, kidney, pericardium

Chakra: heart

Mohs hardness: 6.5–7

Element: earth

Properties: heart expansion, grounding, stability, releasing bad habits

Unakite is known for its power to guide your heart towards relationships and habits that support a balanced and harmonious life. It encourages genuine connection and stability over short-term satisfaction.

Vanadinite

Organ/meridian: heart, kidney

Chakra: solar plexus, sacral, root

Mohs hardness: 3

Element: fire

Properties: sexuality, creativity, vitality, courage

Vanadinite encourages energy to flow to your lower chakras, associated with security, pleasure and creativity. It enhances your life-force energy, promoting determination and passion.

Watermelon tourmaline

Organ/meridian: liver, heart, spleen, kidney

Chakra: heart

Mohs hardness: 7–7.5

Element: water

Properties: love, balance, harmony, emotional healing

Watermelon tourmaline encourages positivity while dissipating negative energy and stress. It promotes an open heart while fostering love, compassion and balance in your life.

Zircon

Organ/meridian: lung, liver, heart, stomach

Chakra: crown, third eye, throat, heart, solar plexus, sacral, root

Mohs hardness: 6–7.5

Element: earth, wind, water, fire

Properties: clarity, protection, spirituality, stability

Zircon enhances spiritual growth and promotes deep connection to the divine. Its calming energy facilitates clear thinking and deep meditative states.

Zoisite

Organ/meridian: lung, liver, kidney

Chakra: heart, root

Mohs hardness: 6.5–7

Element: earth, wind, water, fire

Properties: healing, growth, transformation, emotional balance

Zoisite encourages healing through personal growth and awakening while enhancing creativity and helping you to transform your life.

Crystal combinations

Below is a list of powerful crystal pairings, designed to be used to harmonise and magnify the combined crystal energies. When used together they enhance the desired crystal healing effect.

Anxiety and stress: lepidolite, smoky quartz, howlite, shungite

Bringing change: moonstone, moldavite, rutile, meteorite

Clairvoyance: blue chalcedony, celestite, iolite, blue lace agate, charoite

Courage and confidence: tiger eye, ruby, garnet, carnelian, fire agate

Health and healing: jade, amber, turquoise, hematite, bloodstone, clear quartz

Joy: sunstone, opal, pink tourmaline, peridot

Love: rose quartz, rhodochrosite, morganite, kunzite

Luck: aventurine, chrysoprase, pyrite

Manifesting abundance and money: citrine, rutile, Libyan desert glass, aventurine, pyrite

Meditation and balance: blue lace agate, amethyst, fluorite, green calcite

Processing big emotions: larimar, aquamarine, malachite, blue calcite

Protection: black tourmaline, selenite, obsidian, shungite

Psychic enhancement: tanzanite, blue tourmaline, cavansite, quartz, azurite

Rhodochrosite

Rose quartz

Ruby fuchsite

Rutile

Sapphire

Seraphinite

Serpentine

Sodalite

Sugilite

Tanzanite

Tiger eye

Watermelon tourmaline

PART 2

PLANT MAGIC

INTRODUCTION TO PLANT MAGIC

Plants are powerful magic allies that radiate energy that can be used in rituals or simply in your day-to-day life. Our daily lives are ritualistic after all. Most of us follow some kind of routine or sequence through our daily responsibilities. Through these routines you might encounter plant magic more than you realise – from your morning tea, to the plants in your perfume, to the seasoning on your lunch, and the flowers you walk by every day. Plants surround us and fill the air with magic.

If you wish to work with plant magic in a more intentional way, you can choose to grow your own plants or to purchase plants. Choosing plants for their specific energies and using them in a more intentional way amplifies and synergises the magic to its full potential. Plants vary from flowers, to herbs, to vegetables, to trees. From the moment the seed touches the soil the magic begins, and continues in the cycle of the plant's life all the way until it becomes seed again, magnifying and multiplying its magic eternally. Plants really are magnificent things.

Ways that you can work with plant magic are endless. Here are some suggestions to begin you on your plant magic journey.

Get planting

- Start a small herb garden on your windowsill or in your backyard.

- Grow a flower garden filled with flowers that are grouped with similar magical properties to amplify the energies they emit – for example, a protection flower bed filled with lavender and rosemary.

- Grow a veggie patch, connecting with the earth and your

plants, which will eventually nourish your body with the deep intentions sowed.

Drink tea

- You can create custom tea blends based on your desired plant energy.
- Tea ceremonies infuse your tea with intention and help you to foster more mindfulness in your magic making.

Make a herbal tincture

- You can create tinctures and salves with plants to infuse the healing properties of the plants as well as the energetic properties so that they benefit in both mundane and magical ways.

Create an essential oil blend

- Create custom blends of essential oils made of plants that are in alignment with your desired magical correspondences.

- Essential oil blends can be made into skin-safe oils or mists that can be used to enhance your energy, as a perfume, to cleanse your energy, and so on.
- Use an aromatherapy oil diffuser to fill your space with the magic by spreading the plant oils in your space.

Aromatherapy blends

- Abundance: basil, cinnamon, patchouli, vetiver
- Fertility: geranium, patchouli, lavender, clary sage, ylang ylang
- Focus: peppermint, basil, rosemary
- Health: tea tree, lemon balm, cedarwood, pine
- Joy: sweet orange, ylang ylang, geranium
- Love: rose, jasmine, orange, lime, vanilla
- Protection: frankincense, sandalwood, cedarwood, myrrh, rosemary
- Psychic power: bay, lemongrass, mugwort, blue lotus
- Sleep: lavender, cedarwood, frankincense
- Spirituality: frankincense, myrrh, sandalwood, palo santo
- Stress and anxiety: lavender, clary sage, bergamot

Remember to always mix your essential oils with a carrier oil such as jojoba oil or fractionated coconut oil when using your blends on your body. Just because they are made from plant oils does not mean they cannot be harmful. Plants are powerful magically and also in their potency physically. It is best to use a 2 per cent dilution for your essential oils mixed in carrier oils if they are to be used topically, and to do a small patch test if you have sensitive skin.

Dry some herbs

- Collect herbs from your garden and dry them for use in teas, spells, baths and so on.

- Hang bundles of herbs in your home to enhance the energy of the space, ward off negativity and release beautiful smells.

How to dry herbs

Gather bundles of herbs and tie the branches together with a string or elastic. Don't bundle too many, as there needs to be airflow around them to ensure even drying. Less than 10 branches is ideal. Hang the bundles with the stems up and the herbs pointed towards the floor in a dry, cool, dark place. Once they have dried, store them in an airtight container to preserve them until you're ready to use them.

Create a spell

- Herbs can be used in spells in a myriad of ways, from potions, to altar offerings, to use in spell bags and so on.

- There are many spell books that can guide you if you are new to spellcasting, but you can also create your own when you familiarise yourself with the magical powers of plants.

Make botanical jewellery

- Create jewellery made of seeds, wood and other dried plant materials to carry the energy of the plants with you.

- A great example of this is rose petal beads – see opposite.

70 + *A practical guide to* **MAGIC IN NATURE**

How to make rose petal beads

- Place the picked petals from a bouquet of roses on a sheet pan and leave in the sun to dry almost entirely, to a point where the petals have shrunk but still retain some moisture.

- Using a mortar and pestle or a blender, grind the petals down until they become paste-like. If they do not form a paste, add tiny bits of water until you get the desired consistency.

- Once you have your mixture, grab a small dollop of rose paste and pinch it in your hands, compacting it together and slowly rolling it into a round ball shape about the size of a large pea. Keep in mind that the bead will dry and shrink, so make sure to create a ball slightly larger than you want it to be when finished. As you create the beads you may find you need to squeeze out excess water as you go.

- Run a needle through your bead, and keep it placed within the bead so that the hole retains its shape as the bead shrinks and dries. You will later be able to thread your bracelet or necklace by running a thread through this hole.

- Leave the beads to dry for one to two weeks, occasionally turning to ensure even drying and shape retention. As they harden, give them gentle turns on the needle so that they are not difficult to remove when fully dried.

Be a kitchen witch

- Incorporate magical plants into your cooking by intentionally choosing herbs and vegetables.

- Bless your food while preparing it to enhance its healing properties or nourishment qualities.

Bone broth for physical and energetic health

Making a broth is like making a potion – combining all of the wonderful healing plants and letting them boil to create a healing concoction that flavours your food, soothes your soul, charges your energy and heals your body.

Furthermore, by using kitchen scraps such as leftover bones and vegetable cuttings, you're creating something sustainable, reducing kitchen waste and truly showing intention and gratitude for the ingredients you have and the meals you create.

The beautiful thing about making broths is that you can add whatever you want, according to your desired energetic outcome. Set your intentions as you stir your ingredients together to imbue the broth with your magic.

Start with this base. In a large pot, fill it three-quarters of the way with:

- bone scraps, if you eat meat

- vegetable scraps

- herbs and spices

- a teaspoon of apple cider vinegar

- water to cover.

Simmer the pot uncovered for a minimum of 5 hours, and up to 12 hours if it contains bones or 1 hour if only using plants. Check your broth from time to time to see if it needs more water added or there is any skin/film forming, which will need to be scraped off the top.

Strain the broth, and once it has cooled you can separate into smaller batches to add to your freezer to use over time.

Here are some examples of herbs and ingredients you can consider including in your broth to bring certain magical qualities to your cooking.

Protection

Salt, bay leaf, chilli, rosemary, onion, garlic

Love attraction

Apples, barley, basil, cinnamon, cloves, coriander, ginger, leek, lemon, rosemary, thyme

Improving fertility

Carrot, mustard powder, olive oil

Health and wellness

Bay leaf, garlic, onions, mint, olive oil, rosemary, thyme

Grow some house plants

- Fill your home with plants to bring their magic into the home.

- Fresh bouquets of flowers can fill your space with a beautiful aroma and also the magical energy of the flowers.

- Plants added to your altar can be used to represent the element of earth.

- Cactus plants can be placed around your home to ward off negativity and protect your home.
- A jade plant at your door can attract abundance and wealth.

Have a herbal bath

- Create a ritual out of your bath time by adding intention and specifically chosen botanicals to enhance the energy of your bath, turning your mundane daily cleaning into a blessed purification ritual.
- You can also tie dried botanicals to your shower head if you do not have a bath.
- Be sure to select plants that are safe to use on your skin and will not cause irritation.

Herbal bath blends

Manifesting

Coconut milk powder, bay leaves, rosemary, orange slices

Full moon bath

Coconut milk powder, lavender, rose, cornflower

Psychic power bath

Coconut milk powder, cornflower, sacred lotus

Protection

Coconut milk powder, Himalayan pink salt, Dead Sea salt, rosemary, mugwort

Attracting love bath

Coconut milk powder, roses, apple slices, orange slices

New moon bath

Coconut milk powder, Epsom salts, chamomile, lavender

HOW TO READ THE PLANT PROFILES

In the following sections, each plant profile will contain some or all of the following entries.

Name, botanical name and common name

As the title suggests, this entry is simply the name of the plant, as well as its official botanical name and any other names it is commonly known as.

When buying herbs and plants, it's worth noting that they may be known under a different name in various parts of the world. To ensure you're getting exactly what you need, it's important to take note of the botanical name.

Celestial body

The planets have long been known for their role in governing various aspects of nature, including plants. This section specifies the celestial body associated with each plant. The governing celestial body influences its magical properties. For a deeper understanding of the magical connections between plants and other celestial bodies, refer to Part 4, page 186.

Day

This is the day of the week that corresponds with the plant according to the celestial body that governs it. This is useful to know if you have plans to prepare a ritual with plants on a particular day of the week, and wish to choose plants that are in alignment with that day. Despite the complementary

76 ÷ *A practical guide to* **MAGIC IN NATURE**

nature of using plants on their governing days, you shouldn't feel restricted to using them exclusively on those days.

Element

Earth, wind, water and fire – these elements make up all of nature. Some plants are more significantly influenced by a specific element than others. When this happens, the element influences the magical properties of the plant. For a deeper understanding of the magical correspondences between elements, refer to Part 5, pages 206 to 209.

Energy profile

Energy profile refers to whether the plant falls into an 'active' or 'nurturing' role. In some publications these attributes may be referred to as 'male' and 'female' or 'masculine' and 'feminine'. I have always found it strange to assign gender to plants when discussing their magical correspondences, especially considering those genders are not applicable in the biological structure of the plants. In fact, biologically, most plant species are monoecious, meaning they have both 'male' and 'female' reproductive organs.

When spiritual teachers, writers and content creators assign certain energies to the 'masculine' and 'feminine', they are inadvertently reinforcing stereotypes about how men and women should behave, whether or not they intend to.

The association of strength and assertiveness with the masculine, and similarly the association of nurturing and passiveness with the feminine, further perpetuates the already ingrained societal beliefs that these traits are inherently tied to gender, which is not true. This binary thinking ignores the complexity of human identities and experiences, making spiritual communities unequal and unsafe spaces for people who do not adhere to these gender stereotypes. It's important that spiritual spaces are not used to further establish hierarchical structures of patriarchy, and that spiritual leaders reevaluate the way that they use these terms and deepen their understanding of energy so they don't have to rely on them.

This is why I prefer to not use that language. I feel that 'active' and 'nurturing' are more appropriate words to convey the character of the plant's use.

Characteristics of active plants

Active plants generally emanate qualities such as strength, protection and assertiveness. They have a more active or aggressive energy. In magical applications such as rituals or ceremonies, these plants are often used for courage, protection and manifesting.

Characteristics of nurturing plants

Nurturing plants are, as the name suggests, associated with qualities like receptivity, nurturing and intuition. They are considered to have a more passive or gentle energy. These plants are commonly used in rituals related to love, fertility, enhanced intuition and peace.

Chakra

Plants may resonate with specific energy centres in the body known as chakras. The associated chakra for each plant is listed to help you further understand the relationship between each plant, and how they interact with your body on an energetic level. You can also use this as a guide for selecting a collection of plants for a ritual aimed at a certain energetic need – for example, to make a spell bag filled with heart chakra herbs to help you cultivate love and compassion for yourself.

For a deeper look into chakras, refer to Part 6, page 220.

Magical power

As the title suggests, this entry will explore the specific magical power of that particular plant. This is useful for when you are formulating spells, cooking meals with a specific intention or when you simply want to learn more about the magic of the plants that surround you.

HERBS
AND
SPICES

———

Agrimony

Botanical name: *Agrimonia eupatoria*
Celestial body: Jupiter
Day: Thursday
Element: wind
Energy profile: active
Chakra: third eye, throat
Magical power: protection, induces sleep, hex breaking, wards off evil eye

Agrimony will protect by breaking a hex and returning the energy back to the sender. It protects against the evil eye and banishes negative energy from your space. It is useful in aiding sleep for those who suffer with insomnia and can help to bring overall balance.

Allspice

Botanical name: *Pimenta dioica*
Celestial body: Mars
Day: Tuesday
Element: fire
Energy profile: active
Chakra: solar plexus, sacral
Magical power: health, luck, wealth, anointing, love

Allspice has a rich history of magical properties and has been used for centuries all over South America in everything from food to medicine and even ancient death rituals. This spicy dried berry holds significant luck and prosperity power, and can be used in rituals relating to wealth, abundance and manifesting. It can be used to anoint or bless spiritual items before use in magical work.

Anise

Botanical name: *Pimpinella anisum*
Celestial body: Jupiter
Day: Thursday
Element: wind
Energy profile: active
Chakra: third eye
Magical power: protection, health, power, love

When working with anise, be mindful not to confuse it with the similarly named star anise. Anise is used in rituals for warding off evil spirits. Its sweet fragrance enhances its magical properties for welcoming helpful spirits and attracting lust, love and good fortune. It is also beneficial for decreasing inflammation and improving sleep, making it a wonderful plant to work with for overall healing and well-being.

Basil

Botanical name: *Ocimum basilicum*
Celestial body: Mars
Day: Tuesday
Element: fire
Energy profile: active
Chakra: crown, third eye, throat, heart, solar plexus, sacral, root
Magical power: love, protection, wealth

Basil brings prosperity. It can be used in spell work to promote calm, stress-free energies, and is also known to encourage lust. Hang basil in your home for magical protection and health. The sweet aroma of basil is symbolic of its powerful attracting properties, making it the ideal plant to use when formulating love spells or money spells. It is also beneficial in preparing for spell work, as it can improve mental clarity and focus.

Bay laurel

Botanical name: *Laurus nobilis*
Celestial body: sun
Day: Sunday
Element: fire
Energy profile: active
Chakra: third eye, solar plexus
Magical power: power, health, cleansing, protection

Bay leaves are burned to enhance magical power, psychic ability and manifestation. Bay is used in abundance and prosperity rituals due to its association with success and victory. When used in meditation or dreamwork, bay laurel can invoke prophetic dreams and enhance divine connection.

82 ✢ *A practical guide to* **MAGIC IN NATURE**

BELLADONNA

Botanical name: *Atropa belladonna*
Common name: deadly nightshade
Celestial body: Saturn
Element: water
Energy profile: nurturing
Chakra: third eye
Magical power: psychic power, protection, banishing, visions

Despite its dangerous nature, it is used for its ability to ward off malevolent forces. Belladonna is potent in both its protective qualities, as well as its use in banishing magic. Historically, it has been used to break curses, induce visions and reach transcendental meditative states, although this is now strongly discouraged due to its poisonous nature.

Poison warning: do not ingest. Belladonna is a highly poisonous plant, known as deadly nightshade. Consuming even a small amount of this plant can be fatal.

Bloody dock

Botanical name: *Rumex sanguineus*
Common name: red-veined sorrel
Celestial body: Jupiter
Day: Thursday
Element: wind
Energy profile: active
Chakra: root
Magical power: vitality, courage, personal power

Bloody dock, or red-veined sorrel, has a striking appearance, symbolic of the magical powers it offers: strength and resilience. When used in amulets or spell bags, bloody dock provides vitality and courage to its wearer.

Caper

Botanical name: *Capparis spinosa*
Celestial body: Mars
Day: Tuesday
Element: fire
Energy profile: active
Chakra: sacral
Magical power: aphrodisiac, luck, resilience, influence, potency

Caper is the flower bud of the *Capparis spinosa* plant. It is picked before the flower has opened and then pickled. While most of us know the plant only in its pickled form, you can work with the caper bush flower in either its raw or pickled form. It is used in spells to attract good fortune or to encourage positive change. Its hardy nature is symbolic of its potent power of resilience. Work with the magic of caper when you must endure, and hope to overcome, challenging conditions.

Cardamom

Botanical name: *Elettaria cardamomum*
Celestial body: Venus
Day: Friday
Element: water
Energy profile: nurturing
Chakra: third eye, heart
Magical power: clarity, awakening, love, joy

Cardamom is known for its magical clarity and its ability to aid in enhancing your spiritual practice with sharp focus. Working with cardamom offers support in spiritual awakening, invigorating the mind, body and soul. It is best to work with it when you are doing inner work such as meditation. It can be used in love spells and for attracting joy in your life.

84 ✢ *A practical guide to* **MAGIC IN NATURE**

Chilli pepper

Botanical name: *Capsicum* spp.
Common names: red pepper, hot pepper
Celestial body: Mars
Day: Tuesday
Element: fire
Energy profile: active
Chakra: sacral, root
Magical power: breaking curses, love, passion, protection, banishing

Many types of chilli peppers fall under this category and can be used in the same way, such as cayenne, jalapeño, paprika and serrano chillies.

Chilli is a cherished spice in magical practices due to its immense power and versatility. Use it in spells for love, prosperity and attracting abundance. Its fiery energy is stimulating and invigorating, making it a go-to when you require a little 'warmth'. When used correctly, chilli peppers offer enhanced health, energy, vitality and happiness. When protection is required, turn the heat up to repel ill fortune and malevolent spirits.

Cinnamon

Botanical name: *Cinnamomum verum, Cinnamomum zeylanicum*
Celestial body: sun
Day: Sunday
Element: fire
Energy profile: active
Chakra: solar plexus, sacral
Magical power: prosperity, protection, love, abundance

Cinnamon can bring rapid results when included in your magical practice, as it amplifies energies of other magical elements as well as your power. Use in money spells to attract wealth. Sprinkle at your doorway to invite blessings into your home. The sweet taste of cinnamon is symbolic of its attractive quality, making it a magnet for love, blessings and success.

Cumin

Botanical name: *Cuminum cyminum*
Celestial body: Mars
Day: Tuesday
Element: fire
Energy profile: active
Chakra: solar plexus
Magical power: fidelity, prosperity, relationships, grounding

Cumin seed is known for its use as a money-drawing herb. Use it in prosperity magic to attract wealth and abundance. Cumin seed can also be used to prevent theft or loss of wealth. These magical properties transfer into its use in relationships as a powerful love-attracting herb that also protects against infidelity.

PLANT MAGIC ÷ 85

CLOVE

Botanical name: *Syzygium aromaticum*
Celestial body: Jupiter
Day: Thursday
Element: fire
Energy profile: active
Chakra: throat, solar plexus, root
Magical power: purification, healing, clarity, wealth

Clove is a money-drawing herb, useful in attracting wealth. It is used in rituals for identifying if someone is afflicted with the evil eye and can also be applied to rituals in cleansing and banishing unwanted energetic afflictions. It is a powerful plant, often used medicinally and magically to improve health.

BANISH THE EVIL EYE WITH CLOVES

Take 9 cloves and place them before you. Light a white candle and place a needle into the top of one clove, pinning down into its 'head'. Hold the clove over the flame and set it alight. As it burns say something to the effect of 'Divine spirit, cleanse and protect me.' You can address a particular deity or say a prayer in your chosen religion. Make it personal to you. Discard the clove into a bowl then repeat with the next clove. If a clove makes a popping sound while alight, this signifies that you have been cleansed. Once you have completed this ritual, place the burned cloves into a glass of water, and then blow out the candle. Discard the water and cloves onto the earth outside.

A practical guide to **MAGIC IN NATURE**

Devil's snare

Botanical name: *Datura stramonium*
Common name: jimsonweed
Celestial body: Venus
Day: Friday
Element: wind
Energy profile: nurturing
Chakra: crown, third eye
Magical power: visions, hex
breaking, banishing, psychic power

Datura has a history of use in
shamanic traditions. In magical
practice it is used to invoke visions,
enhance psychic power and
assist you in connecting to the
spirit world. Its potent strength
requires it to be used with respect
and caution. Applied in spells of
protection, devil's snare has the
power to break hexes and banish
unwanted energies, spirits and
entities.

Dill

Botanical name: *Anethum graveolens*
Celestial body: Mercury
Day: Wednesday
Element: fire
Energy profile: active
Chakra: third eye, heart, sacral
Magical power: abundance, love,
luck, wealth

Dill is known for its abundantly
produced seeds, symbolic of its
abundant energy that transfers into
magical power. Utilise this energy

for attracting wealth, love and
prosperity into your life. Whether
used in foods, spells or grown in
your garden, dill will bring you luck
and success in your endeavours.
When used in protection magic,
dill ensures that only well-wishing
energy may enter your presence.

Eucalyptus

Botanical name: *Eucalyptus* spp.
Celestial body: moon
Day: Monday
Element: water
Energy profile: nurturing
Chakra: crown, third eye, solar
plexus, root
Magical power: purification,
healing, mental clarity, protection

This sacred Australian tree
produces incredible magical
power. It is sacred in Indigenous
Aboriginal culture and spiritual
traditions. Eucalyptus leaves are
burned during smoking ceremonies
to bring health and to cleanse away
unfriendly spirits. Eucalyptus leaves
and bark bring good health and
well-being. It encourages mental
clarity and invigorates the mind for
sharp focus.

Grains

Common names: wheat, oats,
barley, rice and so on
Celestial body: Venus

PLANT MAGIC ÷ 87

Day: Friday
Element: earth
Energy profile: nurturing
Chakra: root
Magical power: fertility, grounding, abundance

Grains such as wheat, oats, barley and rice hold significant magical symbolism related to abundance and prosperity. This also translates to them being a wonderful tool for fertility magic. Historically used in magical or spiritual practice, grains have been used in rituals to attract a bountiful harvest or, in modern terms, wealth. This in turn links their magical power to grounded stability and security.

Rice, additionally, can be used in protection and banishing magic. Its absorbent quality is symbolic of the ability to 'soak up' unwanted energies and purify a space. Often used in wedding ceremonies, the throwing of rice is a ritual blessing for abundance and fruitful procreation.

Juniper

Botanical name: *Juniperus* spp.
Celestial body: sun
Day: Sunday
Element: fire
Energy profile: active
Chakra: root
Magical power: protection, purification, cleansing, psychic power

Juniper is a powerful herb that can be used to cleanse away any low energy or unwanted spirits from entering a space. Its berries can be used in spells, incense or on the altar to invoke its power or bring good health. The twigs or branches can be hung in the home or worn as an amulet or talisman for protection. Juniper can also enhance spiritual awareness, making it a useful plant in psychic magic or dreamwork.

Lemon balm

Botanical name: *Melissa officinalis*
Celestial body: moon
Day: Monday
Element: water
Energy profile: nurturing
Chakra: third eye, heart
Magical power: healing, calming, love, tranquillity

Lemon balm is known for its calming and healing properties. It can be used in magic to promote peace, love and harmony. Lemon balm brings success and happiness when used in charms or spells. Use lemon balm in your home to promote health, healing, well-being and tranquillity.

Lemongrass

Botanical name: *Cymbopogon citratus*
Celestial body: Mercury
Day: Wednesday
Element: wind
Energy profile: active
Chakra: solar plexus
Magical power: clarity, focus, protection, psychic ability

Lemongrass is known for its purifying and protective qualities when used in magic. Use it to clear away stagnant or unwanted energies and protect against malevolent spirits. Lemongrass brings focus and clarity to your mind, making it a useful herb to use in meditation, divination and psychic enhancement. Its fresh, uplifting fragrance is symbolic of its magical ability to bring joy and fresh energy into a space.

Marjoram

Botanical name: *Origanum majorana*
Common name: sweet marjoram
Celestial body: Mercury
Day: Wednesday
Element: wind
Energy profile: active
Chakra: third eye, heart, solar plexus
Magical power: happiness, love, emotional well-being, defence

Marjoram is appreciated for its magical properties of love, protection and bringing joy. Use it in spells to dispel negativity in your love life and encourage a deeper love and connection with your partner. Hang it in your home or grow in your garden to create a harmonious and happy environment. Use it in love spells to attract a loving and faithful partner. Marjoram is also helpful for emotional healing, as its gentle energy supports you through hard times.

PLANT MAGIC + 89

Marshmallow

Botanical name: *Althaea officinalis*
Celestial body: moon
Day: Monday
Element: water
Energy profile: nurturing
Chakra: crown, heart, solar plexus
Magical power: healing, compassion, love, psychic power

Marshmallow holds a special place in magical practice for its healing and protective energies. Use it in rituals related to promoting good health, healing from ailments or protecting against harm. Marshmallow root will enhance psychic abilities and dreams. Use it for divination for added power. Marshmallow has a gentle, soothing energy that assists with emotional healing and can enhance your compassion towards others. Its nurturing quality enhances your capacity for universal love and heart expansion.

Mint

Botanical name: *Mentha* spp.
Common names: peppermint, spearmint, wild mint
Celestial body: Mercury, Pluto
Day: Wednesday
Element: wind, fire
Energy profile: active
Chakra: throat, solar plexus
Magical power: prosperity, success, clarity, purification

Mint is known for its invigorating smell and refreshing qualities. This is symbolic of its use in attracting success, abundance and wealth. Use mint in rituals where focus and mental clarity is required. It is an active plant with vibrant energy that zaps away unwanted or stagnant energy, making it useful in spells related to health, happiness and protection.

Nutmeg

Botanical name: *Myristica fragrans*
Celestial body: Jupiter
Day: Thursday

Element: fire
Energy profile: active
Chakra: crown, third eye, heart
Magical power: courage, luck, wealth, protection

Nutmeg is used in magical practice to attract wealth, luck and good fortune. Its warm and spicy energy can be used to invoke a sense of confidence and courage, which can be useful for attracting love, lust and romance! Along with its prosperous energy, nutmeg can also be used to provide protection against dark forces. Use it abundantly for the many blessings it has to offer.

Oregano

Botanical name: *Origanum vulgare*
Celestial body: Mercury
Day: Wednesday
Element: fire
Energy profile: active
Chakra: solar plexus
Magical power: joy, luck, happiness, strength

Oregano has a long history of use in magical tradition. Most notably, it is used for strength and courage in the aftermath of ill fortune. Oregano brings joy and happiness, cleansing spaces of any harmful influence or stagnant energy. It is used to ward off negativity and promotes overall well-being. When used in charms, it enhances your luck. Use oregano in your cooking, on your altar, or in spells to protect, strengthen and uplift.

Paprika

Botanical name: *Capsicum annuum*
Celestial body: sun
Day: Sunday
Element: fire
Energy profile: active
Chakra: root
Magical power: vitality, strength, courage, passion

Paprika is a spice with versatile magical power. Use it in rituals when you need a boost of courage and vitality. Paprika encourages strength and passion and assists in removing blockages or negativity from getting in your way. The vibrant red colour of paprika is symbolic of its properties of love and passion. It can enhance your personal power as well as the power of other magical ingredients.

Parsley

Botanical name: *Petroselinum crispum*
Celestial body: Mercury
Day: Wednesday
Element: wind
Energy profile: active
Chakra: heart
Magical power: protection, purification, health, fertility

PLANT MAGIC ÷ 91

Parsley is a herb most known for its magical use in purifying and protecting. Use it in spells to dispel negative energy and to promote health and wellness. Parsley is believed to attract prosperity and to enhance your fertility. Its fresh smell and vibrant colour is symbolic of the energy it emanates to encourage life, renewal and growth. Use it in your cooking, carry it with you and grow it around your home to enjoy its magical power.

Pepper

Botanical name: *Piper nigrum*
Celestial body: Mars
Day: Tuesday
Element: fire
Energy profile: active
Chakra: root
Magical power: protection, hex breaking, courage, banishing

Black pepper is a potent magical spice used for its protective and banishing properties. Use it in spells to ward off evil and break hexes. Pepper can also be used to enhance the strength or potency of other ingredients in magical practice. Its spicy heat is symbolic of its powerful use to bring courage and assertiveness. Use pepper in your magical practice when you need to enhance your personal power or work on psychic defences.

Red raspberry leaf

Botanical name: *Rubus idaeus*
Celestial body: moon
Day: Monday
Element: water
Energy profile: nurturing
Chakra: sacral
Magical power: fertility, love, healing, attraction

Red raspberry leaf is most notably known for its use in fertility enhancement and pregnancy support. It is also used in spells to protect people during childbirth. Red raspberry leaf will enhance love and attraction and is therefore useful in love spells. It has a nurturing and maternal energy, so it is also useful in spells related to family and supporting healing and overall well-being.

Rosemary

Botanical name: *Rosmarinus officinalis*
Celestial body: sun
Day: Sunday
Element: fire
Energy profile: active
Chakra: crown, third eye, throat, heart
Magical power: mental clarity, memory, purification, protection

Rosemary is venerated in magical practice for its potency and versatility. It has powerful protective, purifying and memory-enhancing properties. Use rosemary in rituals to cleanse spaces or ward off negative energies. Its power in enhancing memory and mental clarity make it ideal for use in spells related to study and focus. Its vibrant energy also supports healing and vitality.

Rue

Botanical name: *Ruta graveolens*
Celestial body: sun
Day: Sunday
Element: fire
Energy profile: active
Chakra: solar plexus
Magical power: psychic enhancement, hex breaking, banishing, protection

Rue had a longstanding history of use in magical practice for its strong protective and banishing power. Use it to ward off evil spirits, break curses, banish negative energy and protect against psychic attack. Rue is a useful herb to work with when you are looking for support in enhancing your psychic abilities and cleansing yourself of unwanted energies. Place rue near new parents and newborns to protect while they are energetically vulnerable in their 'newborn bubble'. Place rue under the bed of someone who is healing to speed recovery.

Saffron

Botanical name: *Crocus sativus*
Celestial body: sun
Day: Sunday
Element: fire
Energy profile: active
Chakra: crown, solar plexus, sacral
Magical power: love, happiness, wealth, mental clarity

Saffron is known for its magical powers of love, happiness and prosperity. Use it in spells to attract wealth and passion. Its vibrant colour is symbolic of its solar energy, which is uplifting to your spirits and encourages courage and abundance. Use it in rituals related to success, joy and manifesting. Its assistance in mental clarity will allow you to finely tune in to your intentions for focused and accurate magic work.

Sage

Botanical name: *Salvia officinalis*
Celestial body: Jupiter
Day: Thursday
Element: wind
Energy profile: active
Chakra: crown, third eye, throat
Magical power: mental clarity, wisdom, purification, healing

Garden sage is a powerful herb in magical practices, known for its use in protection and purification rituals. Use it to cleanse a space, banish unwanted energies and protect against harm. Garden sage is also useful in rituals related to health and well-being, healing and life force. Use sage to enhance your mental clarity and wisdom when embarking on meditative or ceremonial work. Garden sage has a grounding and earthy power that makes it really lovely to work with and brings a sense of stability to your magic work.

St John's wort

Botanical name: *Hypericum perforatum*
Celestial body: sun
Day: Sunday
Element: fire
Energy profile: active
Chakra: crown, solar plexus
Magical power: protection, emotional healing, healing, joy

St John's wort is known for its ability to cure melancholy and bring happiness. Use it to banish negative energies or unwanted spirits and invite in joyful energies. S John's wort carries a bright sunny energy that supports emotional well-being and lifts spirits.

94 ✢ *A practical guide to* **MAGIC IN NATURE**

SALT

> Common name: sodium chloride
> Celestial body: Earth
> Element: earth
> Energy profile: nurturing
> Chakra: root
> Magical power: banishing, cleansing, grounding, purification, protection

Salt is one of the most fundamental elements in magical practices. It is most notably known for its potent purifying and protective properties. It can be used to cleanse spaces, objects and people. It will absorb and neutralise harmful energies. It is one of the most essential ingredients for anyone who wishes to work with the magic of nature. Salt is so revered that is can also be used as an offering to deities and spirits connected to purification, protection and the earth. Below are some ways that you can utilise the magical power of salt.

Bathing: add salt to your bath to cleanse and remove negative energy.

Circles: create a ring of salt around yourself or your space to create a protective barrier. This will prevent any spirits or energies from interfering with your ritual.

Magical tools: place items such as crystals, altar tools, talismans and so on in a bowl of salt to cleanse them.

Salt has historically been so valuable that its availability was symbolic of protection and its power to ward off ill fortune, so much so that across multiple cultures, spilling salt is considered a bad omen – a sign that you have been struck with bad luck or misfortune. To counteract this bad luck, take a small pinch of salt and toss it over your left shoulder to ward off the devil and any other evil spirits who are awaiting the opportunity to wreak havoc.

Star anise

Botanical name: *Illicium verum*
Celestial body: Jupiter
Day: Thursday
Element: wind
Energy profile: active
Chakra: third eye, solar plexus, sacral
Magical power: luck, psychic power, protection, purification

Star anise is known for its power to protect, purify and enhance your psychic power. Use it to cleanses spaces, ward off evil spirits and protect against unwanted energies. Its star shape is symbolic of its connection to higher realms, and as such star anise can be used to strengthen your connection to the divine, enhance your spiritual awareness and help you tap into your innate magical gifts. Star anise is also useful in rituals related to luck and fortune.

Thyme

Botanical name: *Thymus vulgaris*
Celestial body: Venus
Day: Friday
Element: water
Energy profile: nurturing
Chakra: throat, heart, solar plexus
Magical power: protection, purification, courage, prosperity

Thyme is useful in spells and rituals related to protection and abundance. Use it to inspire courage and to promote success and abundance. It has a nurturing energy that gently cleanses away any ill-placed energy and supports healing and growth in its place.

Tobacco

Botanical name: *Nicotiana tabacum*
Celestial body: Mars
Day: Tuesday
Element: fire
Energy profile: active
Chakra: solar plexus
Magical power: spirit communication, grounding, purification, offering

Tobacco is considered sacred across many indigenous cultures. It holds powerful magical properties for protection, purification and communication with the spirit world. As such, tobacco should be used with great reverence.

Tobacco is used as an offering to spirits when seeking their guidance or assistance. The smoke created by tobacco has powerful cleansing properties, ridding away any evil spirits, negative energies or lingering energetic attachments.

While tobacco is connected to the element of fire, it has a deep earthy resonance that makes it a powerful grounding plant. Tobacco's potent connection to the spirit world makes it useful in rituals where you are required to contact spirits or enhance your awareness to beyond the veil of this realm. Its energy is both supportive and transformative. Use wisely.

Violet leaf

Botanical name: *Viola* spp.
Celestial body: Venus
Day: Friday
Element: water
Energy profile: nurturing
Chakra: heart
Magical power: luck, love, healing, peace

Violet leaf is a lovely herb for bringing about love, luck and well-being. Use it in love spells, healing spells and to give you a good luck boost. Violet leaf emanates a soothing energy, making it a supportive plant for promoting peace, tranquillity and harmony.

Wolfsbane

Botanical name: *Aconitum* spp.
Common name: aconite
Celestial body: Saturn
Day: Saturday
Element: water
Energy profile: nurturing
Chakra: root
Magical power: hex breaking, banishing, psychic power, defensive magic

Wolfsbane, also known as aconite, is a potent plant known most for its use in protection and magical defence. Use it to break hexes, cleanse your space, banish evil spirits and protect against negative energies. It is a toxic plant and should be used carefully.

PLANT MAGIC ✦ 97

FLOWERS
AND
SHRUBS

———

ALOE VERA

> Botanical name: *Aloe barbadensis Miller*
> Celestial body: moon
> Day: Monday
> Element: water
> Energy profile: nurturing
> Chakra: solar plexus
> Magical power: healing, soothing, moisturising, protection, beauty

The use of aloe vera in rituals has a long history, dating back as far as ancient Egypt. It was considered the 'plant of immortality', and it is believed that queens Cleopatra and Nefertiti both used aloe vera in their rituals to maintain beauty and youth. Aloe vera was also used in ancient Egyptian embalming rituals, in preparation for the afterlife. Today, it is still considered one of the most popular plant remedies.

To utilise the plant's physical healing properties, apply the gel-like flesh from the leaves of the plant to small cuts, burns and wounds to help heal the injury.

To energetically and magically protect your home from negativity, place living aloe vera plants around your home. They can be placed at your front door, on windowsills or on your altar. The spiked leaves will deter unwanted energy, while the gentle-natured plant will attract soothing and healing energy.

A dying aloe vera plant can be a sign that malevolent energies or spirits are surrounding you, and you need to take stronger action to cleanse your space.

Angelica

Botanical name: *Angelica archangelica*
Celestial body: sun
Day: Sunday
Element: fire
Energy profile: active
Chakra: crown
Magical power: divination, protection, inspiration, blessings, spirituality

Angelica can be used to strengthen your connection to the divine. It is an aid for spiritual expansion and can be used in bids for angelic healing. When used for its protective qualities, angelica can ward off psychic attack, hexes and other magical ill fortune. It can be used to consecrate items, to bring blessings or hung in a home to ensure dark energies are kept at bay.

Angel's trumpet

Botanical name: *Brugmansia* spp.
Celestial body: moon
Day: Monday
Element: water
Energy profile: nurturing
Chakra: third eye
Magical power: spirit communication, visions, protection

Angel's trumpet is known for its power in facilitating communication with the spirit world. The growth of the plant facing downwards is symbolic of a trumpet pointing towards the dead. Historically, it was used to induce visions and encourage a dream state. Use with caution.

Poison warning: do not ingest – angel's trumpet is a poisonous plant.

Arnica

Botanical name: *Arnica montana*
Celestial body: sun
Day: Sunday
Element: fire
Energy profile: active
Chakra: root
Magical power: healing, protection, comfort

Famed for its healing properties, arnica soothes pain and reduces inflammation in physical injuries. Use in rituals or spells related to health, healing and protection to ward off harm and promote well-being.

Astragalus

Botanical name: *Astragalus membranaceus*
Celestial body: sun
Day: Sunday
Element: fire
Energy profile: active
Chakra: root
Magical power: strength, vitality, immunity

Astragalus boosts your strength and life-force energy. It can be used in spells to enhance stamina, encourage resilience and boost your immune system. Use in tea, spell bags, charms or rituals to improve your health and strengthen your magical power.

Blessed thistle

Botanical name: *Cnicus benedictus*
Celestial body: sun
Day: Sunday
Element: fire
Energy profile: active
Chakra: solar plexus
Magical power: healing, protection, purification, blessings

Blessed thistle is used for its power in promoting health and protection. Use it in rituals to cleanse yourself, break curses and guard against negative energy. It can be used in spells or worn on your body to protect from harm and bring blessings into your life.

Blue butterfly pea flower

Botanical name: *Clitoria ternatea*
Celestial body: Venus
Day: Friday
Element: water
Energy profile: nurturing
Chakra: throat
Magical power: calming, love, communication, clarity

Blue butterfly pea flower promotes calmness and clarity of your mind, eliminating stress and brain fog. It encourages communication, making it perfect for spells and rituals relating to truth or expression.

PLANT MAGIC ÷ 101

BLUE LOTUS

> Botanical name: *Nymphaea caerulea*
> Common names: sacred blue lily, blue Egyptian water lily
> Celestial body: moon
> Day: Monday
> Element: water
> Energy profile: nurturing
> Chakra: crown, third eye
> Magical power: spirituality, intuition. visions, tranquillity

Blue lotus is a powerful plant that enhances your spirituality and strengthens your intuition. It has a calming and soothing energy, useful in visualisation or meditation practice. Blue lotus fosters spiritual growth by deepening your connection to the divine and enhancing your psychic power.

Calendula

Botanical name: *Calendula officinalis*
Celestial body: sun
Day: Sunday
Element: fire
Energy profile: active
Chakra: solar plexus
Magical power: happiness, healing, protection, prosperity

Calendula is most known for its powerful skin-healing properties. It has regenerative properties, symbolic of its magical use for promoting health, wellness and uplifted spirits. It promotes positive energy that attracts abundance and blessings.

Cannabis

Botanical name: *Cannabis sativa* or *Cannabis indica*
Common names: marijuana, weed, pot, ganja
Celestial body: moon
Day: Monday
Element: water
Energy profile: nurturing
Chakra: crown
Magical power: relaxation, healing, spiritual expansion

Cannabis is used in rituals to promote meditative states and encourage spiritual expansion. When used responsibly and with intention, it has the power to connect you to higher states of being, heal on a physical and energetic level, and promote positivity.

Carnation

Botanical name: *Dianthus caryophyllus*
Celestial body: sun
Day: Sunday
Element: fire
Energy profile: active
Chakra: heart
Magical power: healing, love, adoration

Carnation attracts love and adoration. It is useful in love spells and rituals for enhancing or improving your relationships. Carnation is also useful in healing rituals, offering strength and health to those who need it.

Castor bean plant

Botanical name: *Ricinus communis*
Common name: castor oil plant
Celestial body: sun
Day: Sunday
Element: fire
Energy profile: active
Chakra: root
Magical power: protection, banishing, healing

Castor has highly protective properties, making it useful for

PLANT MAGIC + 103

banishing negative energies, warding against harm and breaking curses. It draws toxic energy out of your space and offers healing, making it a perfect plant for healing ointments, salves and anointing oils.

Poison warning: castor is a poisonous plant and should be used with caution.

Catmint

Botanical name: *Nepeta cataria*
Common names: catnip, catsmint
Celestial body: Venus
Day: Friday
Element: water
Energy profile: nurturing
Chakra: throat, heart
Magical power: love, happiness, psychic power

Catnip is a happiness-enhancing plant, known for its love-attracting properties. It boosts and nurtures joyful and playful energy. Catnip can be used to amplify your psychic power. Utilise this plant by growing it around your home and in ritual baths, teas or spell bags.

Chamomile

Botanical name: *Matricaria chamomilla* or *Chamaemelum nobile*
Celestial body: sun
Day: Sunday

Element: water
Energy profile: nurturing
Chakra: solar plexus
Magical power: sleep, peace, love, protection

Chamomile is a soothing and calming plant known for promoting peaceful energies. Incorporate it into spell bags, teas, bathing rituals and more to encourage sleep and relaxation. Chamomile can also be used in protection and love-attraction spells and rituals.

Chaste berry

Botanical name: *Vitex agnus-castus*
Common names: vitex
Celestial body: Venus
Day: Friday
Element: water
Energy profile: nurturing
Chakra: sacral
Magical power: balance, fertility, calm

Chaste berry is known for its ability to balance hormones and enhance fertility. Use it in fertility spells and rituals related to reproductive health. Its balancing health properties are symbolic of its magical power to balance and bring about calmness and harmony.

Chrysanthemum

Botanical name: *Chrysanthemum* spp.
Celestial body: sun
Day: Sunday
Element: fire
Energy profile: active
Chakra: solar plexus
Magical power: protection, good fortune, luck

Chrysanthemum is a powerful protective flower known for its use in spells and rituals to guard against negative forces, promote safety and safeguard when offered to deities. It promotes good fortune and luck, enhancing the positive energy in your space.

Cornflower

Botanical name: *Centaurea cyanus*
Celestial body: Venus
Day: Friday
Element: water
Energy profile: nurturing
Chakra: throat
Magical power: psychic power, healing, love

Cornflower can be used in love spells and rituals to attract or improve romance in your life, as well as in magic related to health and well-being. Its deep indigo hue is indicative of its powerful third-eye energising powers, enhancing your psychic abilities, connection to the divine and overall magical gifts.

Daffodil

Botanical name: *Narcissus* spp.
Celestial body: Venus
Day: Friday
Element: water
Energy profile: nurturing
Chakra: solar plexus
Magical power: rebirth, luck, love

Daffodil brings luck. It is useful in spells for love and fertility. Its association with spring time is symbolic of the daffodil's vibrant energies encouraging prosperity, positive change and renewal.

DANDELION

Botanical name: *Taraxacum officinale*
Celestial body: Jupiter
Day: Thursday
Element: wind
Energy profile: active
Chakra: solar plexus
Magical power: wishes, psychic power, mental clarity

Dandelion is a symbol of joy and nostalgia for many, evoking childhood memories of making wishes in the garden while blowing seeds into the wind. When done with intention, this practice can be used to manifest desires while releasing unwanted energies. Dandelion root is a useful magical plant for tea to promote psychic strength and clarity.

Echinacea

Botanical name: *Echinacea purpurea*
Celestial body: Mercury
Day: Wednesday
Element: wind
Energy profile: active
Chakra: solar plexus
Magical power: healing, protection, strength

Echinacea boosts health and healing energies in your body and promotes strength. It is an immune-system booster that offers protection both physically and energetically. It is best used in tinctures, teas and healing spells.

Elderflower

Botanical name: *Sambucus nigra*
Celestial body: Venus
Day: Friday
Element: water
Energy profile: nurturing
Chakra: heart
Magical power: healing protection, love

Elderflower is associated with healing and protection. It can be used in rituals of spell work related to illness or promoting recovery. It has a gentle energy that promotes harmony and love. Elderflower is an easily accessible plant for use in teas, tinctures, baths or even cordials, making its application in magic open for many possibilities.

Feverfew

Botanical name: *Tanacetum parthenium*
Common name: featherfew
Celestial body: Venus
Day: Friday
Element: water
Energy profile: active
Chakra: third eye
Magical power: protection, purification

Feverfew has many health benefits including helping with headaches and migraines. Use it in rituals for decreasing inflammation and pain in your body, reducing your risk of getting sick and for protection against negative energy.

Foxglove

Botanical name: *Digitalis purpurea*
Celestial body: Venus
Day: Friday
Element: water
Energy profile: nurturing
Chakra: heart
Magical power: protection, psychic power, healing

Foxglove's toxic nature makes it useful in protection and defence magic and for warding off negative energies and unwanted spirits. It

PLANT MAGIC + 107

has magic power that can be used in enhancing psychic abilities and also in healing rituals, especially for heart-related issues.

Poison warning: Foxglove is poisonous and should be used with caution.

Heather

Botanical name: *Calluna vulgaris*
Celestial body: Venus
Day: Friday
Element: water
Energy profile: nurturing
Chakra: heart
Magical power: luck, protection, health

Heather is associated with luck and protection. It can be used in spells and charms to bring about good fortune or to ward off ill wishes and negativity. These energies, which enhance your overall wellness and protection in turn, make it beneficial for health and healing rituals.

Hibiscus

Botanical name: *Hibiscus rosa-sinensis*
Celestial body: Venus
Day: Friday
Element: water
Energy profile: nurturing
Chakra: heart
Magical power: love, attraction, divine connection

Hibiscus is often thought of as a plant of lust. Using it in love spells enhances your attraction and luck in romantic partnerships. Hibiscus has a vibrant and nurturing energy that promotes mental clarity and divine insight that is led by the heart.

Honesty

Botanical name: *Lunaria annua*
Common names: moonwort, silver dollar, dollar plant
Celestial body: moon
Day: Monday
Element: water
Energy profile: active
Chakra: heart
Magical power: protection, abundance, honesty

Lunaria, also known as honesty, is named for its moonlike appearance. It produces a seed pod that is used to protect fromevil. The transparent seed pod is symbolic of the magical powers it possesses to bring transparency to situations. Use honesty to illuminate the truth and all potential paths forward. It can be hung in your home, placed on your altar, worn in jewellery or used in spell work to attract abundance, fertility and wealth.

Honeysuckle

Botanical name: *Lonicera* spp.
Celestial body: Jupiter

108 ÷ *A practical guide to* **MAGIC IN NATURE**

Day: Thursday
Element: earth
Energy profile: active
Chakra: heart
Magical power: abundance, protection, psychic power

Honeysuckle brings prosperity and abundance into your life. Use it in spells or rituals to attract wealth and success. It also enhances your psychic ability, bringing clarity and enhanced insight to your divination practice.

Hyssop

Botanical name: *Hyssopus officinalis*
Celestial body: Jupiter
Day: Thursday

Element: fire
Energy profile: active
Chakra: third eye, throat
Magical power: cleansing, protection, health

Hyssop wards against illness and ill wishes. It can be hung in the home to prevent sickness or worn as a protective amulet. It encourages healing when used in rituals related to health and wellness while purifying any negative energy from people and environments.

Jasmine

Botanical name: *Jasminum officinale*
Celestial body: moon
Day: Monday
Element: water
Energy profile: nurturing
Chakra: crown, third eye, heart
Magical power: love, meditation, psychic power

Jasmine is known for its properties of love and spiritual expansion. Its magical power can be used to attract romantic relationships, to enhance psychic power, promote a meditative state and strengthen your connection to the divine.

LAVENDER

Botanical name: *Lavandula*
Celestial body: Mercury
Day: Wednesday
Element: wind
Energy profile: nurturing
Chakra: crown
Magical power: peace, sleep, wellness

Lavender is most known for its power in inducing sleep. Use it in spells or rituals to promote tranquillity, improve insomnia, or to bring balance and harmony. Its relaxing properties make it useful for creating overall wellness in your life. It can also be used in teas, baths and cooking and sprinkled in your pillow case.

Lily

Botanical name: *Lilium* spp.
Celestial body: moon
Day: Monday
Element: water
Energy profile: nurturing
Chakra: crown
Magical power: purity, fertility, renewal

Lily should be used at the beginning of a new cycle to promote renewed energy. When used for fertility, lily fosters growth and transformation. It encourages vibrant, fresh energy that is uplifting and purifies the energy of the environment.

Lily of the valley

Botanical name: *Convallaria majalis*
Celestial body: Mercury
Day: Wednesday
Element: wind
Energy profile: active
Chakra: heart
Magical power: joy, protection, clarity

Lily of the valley can be used to improve mental clarity, help with decision making and assist with memory. It has an uplifting energy that brings joy, making it useful in spells related to happiness and positivity. As with most poisonous plants, lily of the valley has protective power, as its toxic nature deters lingering spirits and eliminates negative energy.

Poison warning: lily of the valley is a poisonous plant and should be used with caution.

Marigold

Botanical name: *Tagetes* spp.
Celestial body: sun
Day: Sunday
Element: fire
Energy profile: active
Chakra: solar plexus
Magical power: protection, strength, intuition

Marigold is known for its protective power, often used to promote safety and ward off negative energies. Its vibrant energy offers hope, strength and healing. Use marigold when you need to enhance your psychic power and attune your intuition.

Milk thistle

Botanical name: *Silybum marianum*
Celestial body: Mars
Day: Tuesday
Element: fire
Energy profile: active
Chakra: solar plexus
Magical power: healing, protection, purification

Milk thistle is known for its healing properties, most notably to improve liver health, strengthen your immune system and reduce inflammation. Its purifying nature makes it useful for spells and rituals related to health, wellness, reducing stress and banishing ill wishes.

Motherwort

Botanical name: *Leonurus cardiaca*
Celestial body: Venus
Day: Friday
Element: water
Energy profile: nurturing
Chakra: heart, sacral
Magical power: peace, protection, health

Motherwort has calming, protective properties, useful in protecting your peace and quiet enjoyment of life. It guards against disruption and negative energy while encouraging health and well-being.

MUGWORT

Botanical name: *Artemisia vulgaris*
Celestial body: Venus
Day: Friday
Element: earth
Energy profile: nurturing
Chakra: crown, third eye
Magical power: psychic power, protection, dreamwork

Mugwort is a powerful psychic enhancer known for promoting prophetic dreams as well as strengthening intuition and inner wisdom. It is useful in spells where extra protection is required, especially from psychic attack, and can also be used to deepen spiritual awareness during meditation. There are many ways to utilise mugwort's protective energies, some of which include burning it to create purifying smoke, hanging it in the house, drinking it as a tea or growing it around your home.

Mullein

Botanical name: *Verbascum thapsus*
Celestial body: Saturn
Day: Saturday
Element: fire
Energy profile: nurturing
Chakra: throat
Magical power: healing, protection, courage

Mullein is known for its health-promoting qualities, especially as an expectorant and lung healer. This healing quality is symbolic of its magical power to expel unhelpful energies from your body and promote overall health. Use mullein in spells or rituals related to confidence, courage and bravery.

Orchid

Botanical name: Orchidaceae
Celestial body: Venus
Day: Friday
Element: water
Energy profile: nurturing
Chakra: heart
Magical power: love, beauty, purity

Orchid is known for its association with love, beauty and strength. Its delicate petals are symbolic of its pure energy, making it useful in spells and rituals related to clearing energy and bringing hope and renewal. It can be used to attract love and improve relationships, as well as enhancing your spiritual awareness. Orchid promotes beauty and confidence, making it useful in glamour magic.

Peony

Botanical name: *Paeonia* spp.
Celestial body: moon
Day: Monday
Element: water
Energy profile: nurturing
Chakra: heart
Magical power: protection, healing, banishing, love

Peony has powerful protective powers that make it beneficial for those who need to guard against spirits, unwanted energies, psychic attack and illness. It is known for its power in expelling evil and entities while inviting happy, loving energies into a space with its sweet aroma. Peony has long been associated with health and healing, often used in rituals for recovery or to prevent injury. Display peony in your home to promote love and wellness while keeping negative forces at bay.

Poppy

Botanical name: *Papaver* spp.
Celestial body: moon
Day: Monday
Element: water
Energy profile: nurturing
Chakra: crown
Magical power: sleep, dreamwork, fertility

The abundance of seeds provided by a single poppy flower is symbolic of the plant's prosperous energy. Utilise this in spells or rituals related to manifesting, fertility and prosperity. Poppy is also useful in promoting sleep and encouraging psychic dreams and restfulness.

ROSE

Botanical name: *Rosa* spp.
Celestial body: Venus
Day: Friday
Element: water
Energy profile: nurturing
Chakra: heart
Magical power: love, beauty, healing

Rose has a powerful association with love and devotion. It can be used in love spells, to improve relationships, to enhance your beauty and desirability and to heal a broken heart. Rose has a nurturing and gentle energy that heals emotions and offers comfort during times of ill ease. Rose is known for minimising inflammation, both physical and energetic, making it useful in spells related to wellness and healing. Its sweet fragrance attracts positive and loving energy into any space where rose is present.

Sacred lotus

Botanical name: *Nelumbo nucifera*
Celestial body: moon
Day: Monday
Element: water
Energy profile: nurturing
Chakra: crown
Magical power: clarity, expanded consciousness, purity

Sacred lotus is a revered plant, known for its deep connection to spiritual expansion and enlightenment. It has a pure energy that fosters clarity and insight, making it a powerful plant ally for meditation and divination. Its gentle energy promotes peace and balance, ridding you of anxieties and fears.

Stinging nettle

Botanical name: *Urtica dioica*
Celestial body: Mars
Day: Tuesday
Element: fire
Energy profile: active
Chakra: root
Magical power: courage, healing, protection

Stinging nettle guards against harm and ill wishes, dissipating negative energies and encouraging good health. It boosts courage and confidence, making it useful in spells or rituals where bravery is required.

Sunflower

Botanical name: *Helianthus annuus*
Celestial body: sun
Day: Sunday
Element: fire
Energy profile: active
Chakra: solar plexus
Magical power: positivity, strength, abundance

Sunflower is a symbol of great strength and happiness. It emanates such vibrant energy and fills a room with joy. Use sunflower in spells to promote positivity and invite sun energy into your ritual. It is a hardy plant with a strong stem, symbolic of its power to promote strength, boost vitality and encourage stability in your life. Its many seeds in a single flower head is a visual reminder of its power to promote abundance.

Vervain

Botanical name: *Verbena officinalis*
Celestial body: Venus
Day: Friday
Element: earth
Energy profile: nurturing
Chakra: crown
Magical power: protection, love, healing

Vervain is known for its protective and healing properties. Use it in rituals to ward against negativity

PLANT MAGIC ✧ 117

and promote health and recovery from sickness or injury. It has a nurturing energy that encourages love and harmony.

Violet

Botanical name: *Viola* spp.
Celestial body: Venus
Day: Friday
Element: water
Energy profile: nurturing
Chakra: crown
Magical power: peace, protection, love

Violet is associated with love and protection. It is useful in love spells or rituals to enhance or improve your relationship. Its nurturing energy promotes healing and peace.

Virginia sneezeweed

Botanical name: *Helenium virginicum*
Celestial body: sun
Day: Sunday
Element: fire
Energy profile: active
Chakra: solar plexus
Magical power: protection, strength, healing

Known for its protection and healing qualities, Virginia sneezeweed guards against harmful energies and encourages strength.

Useful in charms and amulets to enhance your energetic defences.

Wattle

Botanical name: *Acacia* spp.
Celestial body: sun
Day: Sunday
Element: fire
Energy profile: active
Chakra: solar plexus
Magical power: cleansing, protection, vitality

Wattle boosts resilience and encourages strength, stability and vitality. It is known for its purifying properties, as it cleanses away unwanted energies from people and environments.

Wood betony

Botanical name: *Stachys officinalis*
Celestial body: Jupiter
Day: Thursday
Element: fire
Energy profile: active
Chakra: solar plexus
Magical power: protection, purification, healing

Wood betony is known for its purifying properties. When used in rituals and spells, it has the power to cleanse away negative energies and protect against harm. It promotes healing, making it useful in spells related to health and recovery.

118 ÷ *A practical guide to* **MAGIC IN NATURE**

YARROW

Botanical name: *Achillea millefolium*
Common names: milfoil, thousand-leaf
Celestial body: Venus
Day: Friday
Element: water
Energy profile: nurturing
Chakra: heart
Magical power: protection, hex breaking, health

Yarrow has the magical power to ward off evil spirits, ill wishes and negative energies. Hang it in your home to keep the space safe from harm or use it in ritual to break curses and purify. It has a nurturing energy that fosters love and harmony in your home.

FRUITS
AND
VEGETABLES

Apple

Botanical name: *Malus domestica*
Celestial body: Venus
Day: Friday
Element: water
Energy profile: nurturing
Chakra: heart
Magical power: love, healing,
fertility, desire

Apple has long been a symbol of
love, lust, desire and romance. It is
associated with multiple goddesses,
making it a powerful symbol of
the divine feminine, the womb and
female fertility. Apple can be used
in spells and rituals to attract or
improve romantic relationships.

Apricot

Botanical name: *Prunus armeniaca*
Celestial body: Venus
Day: Friday
Element: water
Energy profile: nurturing
Chakra: sacral
Magical power: love, passion,
fertility

Apricot is associated with love
and passion. Use it in spells to
attract romance and reignite the
spark in a stagnant relationship.
The magical power of the apricot
supports fertility and enhances
creative energy. Its properties can
be obtained through the use of the

fruit, its juice, oil, the pit, or even
the leaves and flowers.

Avocado

Botanical name: *Persea americana*
Celestial body: Venus
Day: Friday
Element: water
Energy profile: nurturing
Chakra: heart
Magical power: prosperity, health,
love

Avocado is associated with love
and beauty. This nourishing fruit
promotes good health and a strong
heart, useful for attracting love and
romance. Its richness is symbolic
of its bountiful energy, useful
for promoting abundance and
prosperity.

Banana

Botanical name: *Musa* spp.
Celestial body: Venus
Day: Friday
Element: water
Energy profile: active
Chakra: sacral
Magical power: fertility, prosperity,
resilience

Banana is a symbol of fertility
and prosperity. When planted
near a home, it is said to bring
luck to the household. Its energy
offers protection, guarding

PLANT MAGIC ÷ 121

against bad luck or misfortune. By incorporating banana into your spells or rituals you cultivate an energy of abundance, creative power and resilience.

Beetroot

Botanical name: *Beta vulgaris*
Celestial body: Saturn
Day: Saturday
Element: earth
Energy profile: nurturing
Chakra: heart
Magical power: love, heart expansion, stability

Beetroot is associated with love and heart expansion. Use it in spells to strengthen romantic relationships and open your heart to love. Its energy promotes emotional healing and balance, while beetroot's deep-growingg roots are symbolic of the strength and stability they offer.

Blueberry

Botanical name: *Vaccinium* sect. Cyanococcus
Celestial body: moon
Day: Monday
Element: water
Energy profile: nurturing
Chakra: throat
Magical power: hex breaking, youth, health, protection

Blueberry is a powerful protector of the plant kingdom, useful in spells to break hexes and guard against misfortune. It has a youthful energy that makes it beneficial for rituals related to health and beauty.

Cabbage

Botanical name: *Brassica oleracea* var. *capitata*
Celestial body: moon
Day: Monday
Element: water
Energy profile: nurturing
Chakra: sacral
Magical power: fertility, protection, luck

Cabbage is associated with fertility and luck. Use it in rituals to promote reproductive health. It has a protective energy that is beneficial for healing and recovery from illness. Cabbage leaves placed on the breasts of nursing mothers will prevent mastitis and reduce pain and inflammation.

CACAO

Botanical name: *Theobroma cacao*
Celestial body: Venus
Day: Friday
Element: water
Energy profile: nurturing
Chakra: heart
Magical power: love, pleasure, wealth, spiritual connection

Cacao is revered for its loving and insightful energy. When used in ceremony, cacao uplifts your spirits, opens your perception of pleasure and deepens your connection to yourself, others and your spirituality. It has an abundant energy that encourages gratitude and an openness to receiving blessings.

Cherry

Botanical name: *Prunus avium*
Celestial body: Venus
Day: Friday
Element: water
Energy profile: nurturing
Chakra: heart
Magical power: love, beauty, joy

Cherry is associated with love and beauty. Useful in glamour magic and love spells, cherry enhances your beauty and helps to attract a romantic partner. Its sweet quality promotes happy, joyous energy.

Carrot

Botanical name: *Daucus carota* subsp. *sativus*
Celestial body: Mars
Day: Tuesday
Element: fire
Energy profile: active
Chakra: sacral
Magical power: fertility, passion, vitality

Carrot is known for its grounding energy, offering support and stability. It promotes passion and drive, assisting with enthusiasm and decision making. Carrot is a symbol of fertility, useful in rituals for enhancing reproductive health and vitality.

Corn

Botanical name: *Zea mays*
Celestial body: Venus
Day: Friday
Element: earth

Energy profile: nurturing
Chakra: solar plexus
Magical power: abundance,
protection, fertility

Corn is a symbol of abundance
and fertility. Use it in spells to
attract wealth and promote
reproductive health. It is a sturdy
crop that promotes protective and
sustained energy during times of
hardship.

Cranberry

Botanical name: *Vaccinium
macrocarpon*
Celestial body: moon
Day: Monday
Element: water
Energy profile: nurturing
Chakra: sacral
Magical power: protection, healing,
purification

Cranberry is known for its
powerful physical healing
properties. Rich in antioxidants,
it protects against infection
and improves heart health.
Use cranberry in spells or rituals
for healing, recovery and overall
well-being. Its purifying qualities
make it useful in cleansing
spells and for protecting against
unwanted energies.

Cucumber

Botanical name: *Cucumis sativus*
Celestial body: moon
Day: Monday
Element: water
Energy profile: nurturing
Chakra: sacral
Magical power: healing,
purification, fertility

Cucumber has a cooling energy
that promotes healing and
purification. Use it in rituals for
promoting cleansing and health.
Its energy supports fertility and
youth, encouraging growth and
lively power.

Devil's claw

Botanical name: *Harpagophytum* spp.
Celestial body: Mars
Day: Tuesday
Element: fire
Energy profile: active
Chakra: solar plexus
Magical power: protection,
strength, healing

Devil's claw is a powerful protective
plant known for its use in defensive
magic. Use it to drive away evil
spirits and guard against unwanted
energies. It has a vitality-improving
energy that boosts your strength
and resilience. These qualities can
also be utilised in healing spells.

PLANT MAGIC ÷ 125

FIG

Botanical name: *Ficus carica*
Celestial body: Jupiter
Day: Thursday
Element: fire
Energy profile: active
Chakra: sacral
Magical power: fertility, wealth, health

Fig is a symbol of fertility and wealth, helping you connect with your desires so you can manifest them. Use fig in spells or rituals to attract abundance and support reproductive health. It can boost vitality, making it useful for enhancing health.

Fennel

Botanical name: *Foeniculum vulgare*
Celestial body: Mercury
Day: Wednesday
Element: fire
Energy profile: active
Chakra: solar plexus
Magical power: protection, health, courage

Fennel is known for having protection and healing properties. It can be used in rituals or spells to guard against harm, improve health and recover from illness. Fennel boosts confidence and bravery, making it useful in courage-enhancing rituals.

Garlic

Botanical name: *Allium sativum*
Celestial body: Mars
Day: Tuesday
Element: fire
Energy profile: active
Chakra: solar plexus
Magical power: protection, strength, banishing, health

Garlic is renowned for its powerful protection and healing properties. Use it in rituals to ward off negative energies and promote health. Garlic can be used to banish evil spirits or entities from your body, home or environment. It has potent healing powers, useful for boosting immunity, enhancing vitality, fostering strength and healing from illness.

Ginger

Botanical name: *Zingiber officinale*
Celestial body: Mars
Day: Tuesday
Element: fire
Energy profile: active
Chakra: solar plexus
Magical power: prosperity, health, protection

Ginger is known for its health-boosting properties. It has a warming quality that protects your health while strengthening immunity, supporting organ function, soothing muscles and calming nausea. It can be used in spells or rituals to speed recovery after illness or injury, as well as protection spells where health is at risk. Its anti-inflammatory properties are symbolic of its energetic ability to soothe situations that have become 'inflamed'.

Grape

Botanical name: *Vitis vinifera*
Celestial body: moon
Day: Monday
Element: water
Energy profile: nurturing
Chakra: sacral
Magical power: abundance, fertility, protection

Grape is a powerful symbol of devotion, abundance and fertility. It can be used in spells or rituals to attract wealth and improve reproductive health and success in pregnancy. Grape can be used in offerings or placed on your altar to attract abundance while also offering protection and stability.

Grapefruit

Botanical name: *Citrus* x *paradisi*
Celestial body: sun
Day: Sunday
Element: fire
Energy profile: active
Chakra: solar plexus
Magical power: prosperity, happiness, vitality

Grapefruit is associated with joy and vibrant energy. It encourages happiness while uplifting the spirits and encouraging a zest for life. Its vitality-enhancing properties make it useful in spells or rituals related to health, well-being and success.

LEMON

> Botanical name: *Citrus limon*
> Celestial body: moon
> Day: Monday
> Element: water
> Energy profile: nurturing
> Chakra: solar plexus
> Magical power: health, purification, protection

Lemon is a powerful purifier, often called upon in spells to cleanse negative energy, undo hexes or banish impeding influences. Its bright and sunny disposition casts away any negative or low-vibe energies from your environment. Lemon can be used both to cast out evil as well as attract happy energy into the home.

SIMPLE LEMON PURIFICATION RITUAL

Place a lemon in a bowl and cut an X into the side of it. While holding the intention of what energies you wish to banish, place salt, pepper and chilli into the flesh of the lemon. You can also stick cloves or nails into the lemon if you feel that the additional power is needed. Leave the lemon in the bowl and let it work its magic.

When you feel it is time to remove the lemon, you can seal it with the wax of a black candle, or tie it closed with a black ribbon and then bury it away from your home.

Licorice

Botanical name: *Glycyrrhiza glabra*
Celestial body: Venus
Day: Friday
Element: water
Energy profile: nurturing
Chakra: throat
Magical power: love, fidelity, influence

Licorice is associated with love and fidelity, as well as sexuality. Use it in spells to attract a romantic partner or to improve an existing relationship. Its intoxicating energy can also aid you in spells or rituals where you wish to influence or convince someone by enhancing your skills of persuasion and communication.

Lime

Botanical name: *Citrus aurantiifolia*
Celestial body: sun
Day: Sunday
Element: fire
Energy profile: active
Chakra: solar plexus
Magical power: purification, protection, healing

Lime is known for its purifying and protective qualities. It can be used in spells or rituals to cleanse negativity and to promote good health. Lime can be placed around your home to prevent bad luck and to invite happy energies.

Mulberry

Botanical name: *Morus* spp.
Celestial body: Mercury
Day: Wednesday
Element: wind
Energy profile: active
Chakra: throat
Magical power: wisdom, protection, transformation

Mulberry is associated with wisdom and transformation. It can be used in rituals to enhance knowledge and connect with your inner knowing, as well as promote personal growth. Grown from a hardy tree, mulberry is symbolic of the strength and security it energetically provides. Use mulberry tree branches, berries or leaves in spells and rituals related to protection and safety.

OLIVE

Botanical name: *Olea europea*
Celestial body: sun
Day: Sunday
Element: fire
Energy profile: active
Chakra: solar plexus
Magical power: peace, healing, protection

Olive is a symbol of peace and healing. The well-known expression 'extending an olive branch' carries a deep meaning of hope, renewal and goodwill. This perfectly exemplifies the magical associations of this powerful plant. Olives, olive leaves and olive oil can all be used in spells or rituals to enhance health, promote healing from sickness or injury, or protect against negative energy.

Used in essential oil blends: olive oil can be used as a carrier oil for essential oil blends, which amplifies any protective or healing properties of the blends.

Used in massage: olive oil can be used to moisturise and massage. Use on your wrists, behind your ears, on your temples, your scalp and hair, and on the soles of your feet to guard against the evil eye and promote good health.

To determine if you have been cursed with the evil eye: place three drops of olive oil into a bowl of water, one on top of the other, to create a larger oil pool on the surface of the water. If the oil stays together as one body of oil you do not have the evil eye. If it separates into many oil blotches on the water surface you may have the evil eye from multiple sources.

To clear the evil eye: say a prayer or an incantation over the water and then using a needle, knife, or scissors, either stab into the oil blotches or use the scissors to cut above the bowl three times. Pour salt over the water and then discard the water/salt mixture.

PLANT MAGIC ÷ 131

ORANGE

Botanical name: *Citrus* x *sinesis*
Celestial body: sun
Day: Sunday
Element: fire
Energy profile: active
Chakra: solar plexus
Magical power: joy, purification, abundance

Oranges are associated with joy and purification. They can be used in spells or rituals for cleansing negative energies and promoting happiness. They also enhance luck, making them useful in love spells and for attracting wealth and prosperity.

WEALTH-ATTRACTING SPELL

Cut one-third of an orange off the top and then sprinkle the remaining two-thirds of the orange with ground cinnamon and basil. Place the orange in a fireproof dish and then place a small green candle into the centre of the orange. While holding a focused intention for attracting wealth, recite an incantation or prayer. Light the candle and let it burn the whole way down.

Onion

Botanical name: *Allium cepa*
Celestial body: Mars
Day: Tuesday
Element: fire
Energy profile: active
Chakra: solar plexus
Magical power: protection, healing, abundance

Onion is known for its protective and healing properties. Used to ward off evil and to promote good health, onion's energy can be used to attract abundance and vitality, enhancing your strength and resilience. Burn dried onion skins to attract money and place onion around the home to protect your home from negativity and illness. Hang an onion in the bedroom of someone who is ill to remove their illness.

Peach

Botanical name: *Prunis persica*
Celestial body: Venus
Day: Friday
Element: water
Energy profile: nurturing
Chakra: heart
Magical power: love, fertility, protection

Peach is known for its protective energy and association with love and fertility. Carrying a peach pit will offer protection from negative energy, while eating peach will enhance your reproductive health and romantic attraction. Peach can be used in spells and rituals to promote vitality and wellness.

Pear

Botanical name: *Pyrus* spp.
Celestial body: Venus
Day: Friday
Element: water
Energy profile: nurturing
Chakra: heart
Magical power: love, healing, prosperity

Pear is a symbol of love and abundance. It carries magical power that attracts a romantic partner and enhances your capacity to love. Pear can promote well-being and good health and is therefore useful in spells and rituals related to healing.

Persimmon

Botanical name: *Diospyros kaki*
Celestial body: Venus
Day: Friday
Element: water
Energy profile: nurturing
Chakra: sacral
Magical power: love, luck, protection

Persimmon is associated with love and luck. It can be used in spells and rituals to attract romance and good fortune. It can also be used in manifesting spells and money-drawing spells, as persimmon harnesses powerful abundance magic. It also offers protection from illness.

Pineapple

Botanical name: *Ananas comosus*
Celestial body: sun
Day: Sunday
Element: fire
Energy profile: active
Chakra: solar plexus
Magical power: prosperity, healing, strength

Pineapple is a symbol of prosperity and healing. It has the power to boost your vitality, encourage health and offer strength for your immune system and spirit. Pineapple offers regenerative properties, assisting in your ability to recover after illness or ill fortune. The hard outer skin is symbolic of the protection properties it carries. Use pineapple skins and leaves in protection rituals.

Potato

Botanical name: *Solanum tuberosum*
Celestial body: moon
Day: Monday
Element: earth
Energy profile: nurturing
Chakra: root
Magical power: protection, banishing, grounding

Potato has a stable, grounding energy that can offer comfort and security. Potato is a nightshade plant that grows underground and is therefore associated with the underworld and death. This power can be used for casting away energies, bad habits or people out of your life. Potato offers protection and can be used in kitchen witchery or in spell work to guard against negativity and ill fortune.

134 ✦ *A practical guide to* **MAGIC IN NATURE**

POMEGRANATE

Botanical name: *Punica granatum*
Celestial body: Mercury
Day: Wednesday
Element: fire
Energy profile: active
Chakra: root
Magical power: fertility, wealth, protection, intuition

Pomegranate harnesses powerful abundance energy. Its many seeds are symbolic of the abundance it offers in its magic. This can be utilised for boosting fertility, attracting wealth, supporting success and granting wishes. Sprinkle pomegranate seeds at your doorstep to welcome blessings into your home. Use any part of the fruit on your altar as an offering.

Pomegranate also boosts your intuitive power and guards against negative energy, making it useful in protection spells, psychic enhancement and warding against psychic attack.

PUMPKIN

Botanical name: *Cucurbita pepo*
Celestial body: moon
Day: Monday
Element: water
Energy profile: nurturing
Chakra: sacral
Magical power: abundance, fertility, healing

Pumpkin is a symbol of hope, abundance and fertility. It can be used in spells to attract wealth and promote reproductive and general good health. Its healing energy promotes speedy recovery from illness and injury while promoting comforting and grounding energies.

THE MAGICAL HISTORY OF PUMPKIN CARVING

The tradition of carving pumpkins at Halloween, known as jack-o-lanterns, is derived from the ancient Celtic celebration of Samhain. During this festival, which marks the end of the harvest season, the veil between worlds is at its thinnest, which allows spirits to cross over. To ward off evil spirits and protect their homes, people carved faces into turnips and placed them outside. This tradition migrated to America, where pumpkins were native and ideal for carving. Carved pumpkin faces offer protection from unwanted spirits, while the candlelight placed inside the pumpkin offers a light to your ancestors to help them find their way home.

Raspberry

Botanical name: *Rubus idaeus*
Celestial body: Venus
Day: Friday
Element: water
Energy profile: nurturing
Chakra: sacral
Magical power: love, protection, health

Raspberry is known for its use in enhancing love and attraction, and bringing happiness, gentleness and kindness into a home. It has a nurturing energy, so is useful in spells related to family, home, supporting healing, and overall well-being.

Strawberry

Botanical name: *Fragaria* x *ananassa*
Celestial body: Venus
Day: Friday
Element: water
Energy profile: nurturing
Chakra: heart
Magical power: love, luck, desire

Strawberry is associated with love and fertility. Used to enhance luck, attract romance and increase someone's desire for you, strawberry can also promote reproductive health. These qualities can also help attract friendship, kindness, joy and other kinds of 'sweetness' into your life.

Tomato

Botanical name: *Solanum lycopersicum*
Celestial body: Venus
Day: Friday
Element: water
Energy profile: nurturing
Chakra: heart
Magical power: love, protection, healing

Tomato is a symbol of love and protection. As a member of the nightshade family, it is associated with banishing evil spirits and guarding against negative energy. Tomato offers protection and abundance when planted around your home, and when used in cooking it promotes good health and love.

PLANT MAGIC ⁕ 137

ROOTS,
RESINS
AND
WOODS
——

Ashwagandha root

Botanical name: *Withania somnifera*
Celestial body: sun
Day: Sunday
Element: fire
Energy profile: active
Chakra: solar plexus
Magical power: vitality, strength, endurance, clarity

Ashwagandha is known for its powerful properties as an adaptogen. The root in a powdered form is used to support stress relief and enhance mental health. It can be taken as a supplement for immune support or used in ritual spell work to enhance strength, power and mental clarity. To incorporate it into ceremonies, a small amount can be stirred into coffee, tea or cacao.

Calamus root

Botanical name: *Acorus calamus*
Celestial body: moon
Day: Monday
Element: water
Energy profile: nurturing
Chakra: throat
Magical power: healing, protection, balance, wealth

Calamus is associated with healing and protection. Use it in spells to promote recovery and ward against ill wishes and evil spirits. Calamus root enhances your mental clarity and fosters balance and harmony, making it useful in grounding rituals and magical work related to restoring order. It encourages truthful communication, breaks curses and can be used to regain control of a situation.

Dragon's blood resin

Botanical name: *Daemonorops draco*
Celestial body: Mars
Day: Tuesday
Element: fire
Energy profile: active
Chakra: root
Magical power: protection, purification, power

Dragon's blood resin enhances the power of those who use it and the ingredients it is mixed with in magical workings. Use it to strengthen your intention and amplify your rituals. It has powerful protective and purifying properties, making it useful for cleaning, warding off bad energy and warding against evil.

Frankincense resin

Botanical name: *Boswellia sacra*
Celestial body: sun
Day: Sunday
Element: fire
Energy profile: active
Chakra: crown
Magical power: purification, protection, spirituality, consecration

Frankincense is known for its powerful connection to the divine. It can be used in religious ceremonies to consecrate a space and bless items, or used in spiritual rituals to strengthen your connection to the spirit world. Frankincense holds an extremely high vibrational frequency that eliminates lower vibrations from a space. As such, evil spirits and bad energy are purified in the presence of frankincense, making it highly protective.

Ginseng root

Botanical name: *Panax ginseng*
Celestial body: sun
Day: Sunday
Element: fire
Energy profile: active
Chakra: solar plexus
Magical power: vitality, strength, endurance

Ginseng is renowned for its vitality-enhancing properties. It can be used in rituals or spells to boost your strength and endurance. By providing support for your life-force energy, it promotes overall health and well-being, making it useful in rituals related to healing and recovery.

Myrrh resin

Botanical name: *Commiphora myrrha*
Celestial body: moon
Day: Monday
Element: water
Energy profile: nurturing
Chakra: root
Magical power: protection, healing, spirituality

Myrrh is known for its protective and healing properties. It can be used in spells or rituals to safeguard against negativity or to promote health and wellness. Its high vibrational energy supports spiritual connection, making it a powerful meditation and prayer tool.

PALO SANTO

> Botanical name: *Bursera graveolens*
> Celestial body: Mercury
> Day: Wednesday
> Element: wind
> Energy profile: nurturing
> Chakra: third eye, root
> Magical power: purification, protection, spirituality.

Palo santo, which translates to 'holy wood', is a tree with deep spiritual significance. When the tree naturally falls or dies and rests on the forest floor for many years it accumulates a highly fragrant oil, which signifies its spiritual use and power. Palo santo can be burned to create a purifying smoke that eliminates bad energy or used as an essential oil for protection and grounding. When working with palo santo, give thanks to the spirit of the tree and use it with reverence and respect.

Sandalwood

Botanical name: *Santalum album*
Celestial body: Venus, moon
Day: Friday, Monday
Element: water
Energy profile: nurturing
Chakra: third eye
Magical power: purification, protection, spirituality

Sandalwood is known for its purifying and protecting properties. Use it in rituals to cleanse negative energies and ward against harm and ill wishes. Its energy will enhance your spiritual connection, making it a powerful tool for psychic development, meditation and prayer.

Turmeric root

Botanical name: *Curcuma longa*
Celestial body: sun
Day: Sunday
Element: fire
Energy profile: active
Chakra: solar plexus
Magical power: purification, protection, prosperity

Turmeric has a purifying and protective power that lends it to its use in cleansing rituals and ridding your body, life or environment of toxins. Its natural anti-inflammatory qualities make it useful in spells or rituals related to health and healing. Turmeric can be used to enhance your abundance, offering good luck to those who utilise this prosperous plant in magical workings.

MANDRAKE ROOT

> Botanical name: *Mandragora officinarum*
> Celestial body: Mercury
> Day: Wednesday
> Element: fire
> Energy profile: active
> Chakra: root
> Magical power: protection, fertility, power

Mandrake is associated with powerful protection and fertility properties. Used in spells, it has the power to protect you from harm or to promote reproductive health. Use it in love spells to attract a romantic partner, carry in a spell bag as an amulet for protection and luck or place it in a money bowl to amplify your wealth.

Poison warning: mandrake is a poisonous plant and should be handled with care and caution. It should never be ingested.

PLANT MAGIC ✧ 143

PLANTS FOR FERTILITY

PLANTS FOR PROTECTION

Juniper berries
(*Juniperus* spp.)

Rue
(*Ruta graveolens*)

Lily of the valley
(*Convallaria majalis*)

Rosemary
(*Rosmarinus officinalis*)

PLANTS FOR LOVE

Licorice
(*Glycyrrhiza glabra*)

Strawberry
(*Fragaria* x *ananassa*)

Apple
(*Malus domestica*)

Cinnamon
(*Cinnamomum verum*)

PLANTS FOR STRESS RELIEF

PART 3

ANIMALS

INTRODUCTION TO ANIMAL MESSENGERS

It is often said that when an animal appears to you unexpectedly, it has been guided by the spirit of one of your ancestors, beckoning it to visit you in order to pass on a message that they are with you. In this instance, the animal acts as a companion and messenger from our loved ones beyond the veil.

Animals are magical creatures of nature, and therefore they also often bring their own messages to you, guided by their innate wisdom. Sometimes the message is their mere presence and of their own merit. Other times, you may intuitively or psychically receive a message from an animal when you encounter them – either in waking life or in your dreams. Animal symbolism is deeply rooted in many different spiritual and cultural beliefs around the world from which these meanings have been derived. When we study the significance and meaning of each animal, we are better able to interpret these messages. While there are more than 50 animals listed in this section of the book, you may come across an animal messenger in your journey that is not listed here. If this happens, look for the animal that most closely matches your messenger's physical appearance and characteristics. The magic of animal messengers is intrinsically linked to their behaviours, appearance, capabilities and habits.

Animal correspondences can be used to:

- interpret the meanings of dreams where animals are present

- call upon the spirit of the animal when you require its specific qualities

ANIMALS ÷ **153**

- seek guidance from animals that you feel an affinity to during meditation
- place animal totems in grids, vision boards, spell bags or on your altar when you wish to summon the power of a particular animal.

Each of the animal entries in this section offers keywords and a message from the animal. The keywords on each entry allow you to interpret the spiritual meaning of an animal at a glance. For a more in-depth understanding, look towards the animal message.

ANIMALS A–Z

Ant

Keywords: community, teamwork, strength, discipline

The ant is known for its surprising strength, discipline and ability to work together for the benefit of the colony. Each ant plays a vital role in the community, demonstrating that every ant's action, no matter how small, has a significant impact.

Focus on your goals with persistence and patience. The ant reminds you to be disciplined and always remember that your actions affect others. Be reliable and dependable for those who need you. If you don't yet have a team or community to turn to, the ant could be urging you to find that community. It's also important to consider how you can work within your community towards shared goals.

Bear

Keywords: strength, healing, introspection, inner power, solitude, courage

The bear is known for its size, strength and sense of family. When we visualise a bear, many of us would instinctively think of a mamma bear protecting her cubs or a bear in hibernation. These themes of self-care and relationship are carried through to the magical meaning of bear when it appears to you as a messenger.

Embrace your inner strength and protect what is important to you. Take time for solitude and introspection. Rest is a crucial part of life and necessary for your overall well-being. When the bear appears you're asked to prioritise your health or take actions towards healing. You're encouraged to be courageous, nurture your loved ones and stand your ground.

ANIMALS ✣ 157

BEE

> Keywords: community, productivity, fertility, sweetness

The bee works in a community, each member with its own important role vital to the functioning of the collective. The bee plays a critical role in our ecosystem as it is responsible for pollination and honey production, without which we would not be able to grow crops for food. The harmony of the bee world is maintained because each bee works diligently towards that sweet honey goal.

Embrace transformation, knowing that all the hard work will result in a sweet reward. Think about what you are 'pollinating' in your life, where your energy is being spent and what your efforts are working towards. The bee is a messenger of abundance and life. Working with bee energy can help with fertility and manifesting.

If you feel that your individual role in society is not significant, remember that like the bee you play a vital role, and that role helps to maintain balance in your environment. Foster harmony in your home and life, especially during times of chaos. It's important to maintain order and organisation. Focus on your community and relationships. When you work together you can achieve more and also feel supported.

BEESWAX CANDLE MAKING

Making beeswax candles is easy! They have a cleaner burn than most commonly sold candles, which include toxic additives like petroleum, making them a healthy candle option for people who are living a toxin-free lifestyle. Beeswax candles are also eco-friendly as they use non-synthetic chemicals, and have minimal environmental impact.

Beeswax sheets can be purchased from local beekeepers, craft stores and many online sellers.

Lay a flat sheet of beeswax on a clean work surface.

Place a candle wick along the edge of the sheet.

Gently warm the wax sheet until it is malleable using either sunlight or a low setting on a hairdryer in small increments.

Fold the thin edge of the wax over the length of the wick and press into the wick to secure it.

Gently roll the sheet around the wick, firmly pressing and securing the end of the sheet to stop it from unravelling.

Your beeswax candles are now ready to use. Use beeswax candles in spell work where you want to incorporate the energy of bees.

BEETLE

> Keywords: transformation, regeneration, protection, renewal

The beetle comes in all shapes and sizes but each has one thing in common – its hard exoskeleton. Some are seen as garden pests, while others are known for their benefits in a garden as they eat more harmful pests. Despite its small size, the beetle is often one of the key identifying factors of biodiversity in an environment, as it only appears in areas with a healthy ecosystem. Some entomologists consider the beetle the most important organism on our planet because of this.

Embrace change, and adapt to your new environment with resilience. Renewal is always possible. The beetle reminds you to trust in your ability to overcome any challenge. Like a beetle who burrows into the earth, take time to ground yourself.

In ancient Egypt, the scarab beetle carried special significance. It symbolises rebirth and protection. Amulets were created in the image of the scarab to help protect the dead and aid them in their journey to the afterlife. The scarab beetle's life cycle served as a metaphor for regeneration.

Bird

Keywords: peace, freedom, spirituality, higher knowing

The bird embodies the very essence of the wind element, as it effortlessly soars through the air. The wind element is associated with your thoughts, intellect and imagination. The bird symbolises freedom, liberation, limitless potential, spiritual messages and connection to the divine.

We can work with the energies of the bird in many ways, such as going bird watching, using images of birds, calling on bird spirits, or using ethically sourced bird parts such as feathers, eggs and bones as ritual tools.

Feathers symbolise freedom, spirituality and higher knowing. Finding a feather can be a sign that your guardian angels are with you. It can also be a sign that a loved one who has passed away is visiting you.

Bones from some birds can be used in broths, to nourish your body, or used in divination – think wishing bones from chickens and bone casting. They can symbolise death, unity, the cyclical nature of energy and connection to the divine. You can also place ethically sourced bird bones on your altar to represent the wind element.

Eggs symbolise birth, life, protection and cleansing. They are often used in fertility, protection, hex-breaking and cleansing spells.

You can source these bird parts ethically by using items that are a byproduct of food production. If you need chicken bones in your spell work, you can collect them after cooking dinner, wash them and then save them for rituals. It is possible to source feathers that have naturally shed, rather than purchasing feathers that have been plucked to meet demand.

While there's much information regarding animal sacrifice in magic and the occult, we must do our best to leave a positive impact on the earth, and not take the creation and life of nature for granted. It is not only worth considering the energetic impact that an act like animal sacrifice would have on our own energy, but it would not be thoughtful nor sustainable to sacrifice a chicken for its bones and then leave the bird to waste.

Buffalo

Keywords: abundance, gratitude, survival, unity, strength, balance

The buffalo encourages you to appreciate all that you have in life. You're asked to observe your life, surroundings and your company, and to draw strength from your connection to others and the earth. Now is a time to cultivate gratitude. Embrace your inner strength, your unity with the world and the abundance that surrounds.

Butterfly

Keywords: transformation, rebirth, innocence, grace, growth, change

The butterfly is a creature of immense beauty, appreciated across the world as a messenger of change and evolution. The butterfly represents resurrection and metamorphosis. Often seen as the symbol of your soul's journey, the butterfly represents our own spiritual evolution through the phases of birth, life, death and rebirth. It also symbolises the immense power of even the smallest action and its possibility to have a ripple effect that initiates significant change. This phenomenon is known more commonly as the 'butterfly effect'.

When the butterfly appears to you, you're being reminded of your immense capacity for expansion and change. You're embarking on a journey of transformation, personal growth and new beginnings. Much like the butterfly emerging from the cocoon, you must trust that, when you spread your wings, you will fly! Let go of the past to make space for what's ahead.

Cat

Keywords: mystery, curiosity, independence, intuition

The cat encourages you to embrace your independence. Whether exploring unfamiliar experiences or exploring the depths of your intuition, the cat asks you to stay curious. Lean into the mystery and cultivate a deeper understanding of yourself and the world around you. Now is a time for self-reflection, relaxation and self-care. When the cat appears to you, you're asked to honour your need for solitude.

162 ÷ *A practical guide to* **MAGIC IN NATURE**

CHICKEN

> Keywords: fertility, protection, prosperity, resourcefulness

The chicken is known for its ability to survive in environments that are not ideal. It is adaptable, making use of whatever resources it can find. It is the bird most often associated with eggs, highlighting its connection to family, birth and abundance.

Be adaptable and make the most of the resources available to you. Protect your 'nest' and tend to your creations and hard work so they may hatch undisturbed by outside predators. There is always potential for renewal and growth in all situations. The chicken appears as a messenger to signal the potential for prosperity when you take advantage of opportunities that are present, rather than waiting for more ideal circumstances.

Chicken wishbones are known for bringing luck or granting wishes. Wishbones can be kept to attract good fortune, used in offerings as gifts to spirits or deities, or used in rituals for their luck-attracting properties.

CHICKEN WISHBONE RITUAL

The most common wishbone ritual involves two people holding one side of the wishbone each. As they pull towards themselves to break the bone in half, they each make a wish in their mind. Whoever ends up with the larger bone will have their wish granted.

Coyote

Keywords: cunning, trickster energy, intellect, humour, joy

The coyote encourages you to approach life with a sense of playfulness and joy. Known for its trickery and ability to adapt in the wild, the coyote asks you to embody that same adaptability by viewing challenge as an opportunity and approaching change with excitement. An unexpected transformation is approaching, and how you respond to it will determine whether you grow or struggle. You must trust your instincts and embrace the unpredictability.

Crow

Keywords: magic, intelligence, prophecy, death, adaptability

The crow is known for its intelligence, loud voice and adaptability. The curious crow has incredible problem-solving skills and can mimic the sound of human voices. Known to collect shiny objects and mate for life, the crow also grieves the loss of loved ones.

Embrace this time of transformation and magic. Be insightful and look beyond the surface of what's happening around you to seek deeper understanding. The crow offers prophecy and change. It is a time for truths to be unveiled. Trust in your intelligence and psychic abilities, allowing them to guide you.

Now is the ideal time to explore your magical gifts, to expand your spiritual awareness and to take special care to protect yourself from psychic attack.

Deer

Keywords: gentleness, intuition, innocence, sensitivity, growth

The deer encourages you to embrace your sensitivity. Your surroundings may shift unexpectedly, but you must control your inner world to maintain a sense of balance and peace. When the deer appears, you're reminded to listen to your inner voice and trust your wisdom and sensitive nature. There will be emotional healing and growth on your path that lies ahead.

Dog

Keywords: loyalty, companion, protection, friendship

Embrace loyalty and faithfulness in your relationships. The dog asks you to honour your friendships and companions with love, protection and support. You're encouraged to cherish the bonds you have with others and foster trust with those you love.

Dolphin

Keywords: joy, playfulness, communication, youthfulness, harmony

Embrace playfulness. The dolphin asks you to communicate with others compassionately so you may gain a deeper understanding. Appreciate the beauty of connection and community by cultivating peace and harmony in your relationships. When the dolphin appears, you are encouraged to approach life with joy and freedom and share your life with others.

Dove

Keywords: peace, purity, divine guidance, love, hope

When the dove appears to you it is a sign to seek balance and harmony, and a reminder that you're divinely protected. Create peace in your life. Foster pure intentions and love in your interactions with others. Keep hope in your heart during times of anguish, and know that there is renewal ahead.

Dragon

Keywords: protection, power, fortune, change, magic

Dragon is known for its fierce presence and sacred knowledge. When the dragon appears to you, you're encouraged to embrace your inner strength and power. Trust in your ability to transform and protect all that is sacred to you. You have deep wisdom within you, awaiting your curiosity. The dragon asks you to look within and access it. The dragon is also known for its connection to hidden treasures. A dragon messenger could also be a sign that fortune is on your side.

Dragonfly

Keywords: transformation, adaptability, new beginnings, fresh starts

The dragonfly symbolises change and adaptability. When it appears to you, you're encouraged to embrace change with grace, as new situations are on your horizon. Let go of the past, it will only get in the way of your growth in the future. Now is a time for shedding the layers of old habits to embrace the new. The dragonfly reminds you to trust your ability to adapt to these new situations, and to always follow your path to joy.

Eagle

Keywords: freedom, power, pride, truth, strength, courage

The eagle is known for its power, strength, keen eyesight and ability to reach great heights. Flying at incredible speeds, it can live for over 30 years. The eagle is an expert hunter, mates for life and is highly intelligent.

Embrace your inner strength to soar above challenges. The eagle appears to you to encourage you to strive for freedom in your life. Look at your situation with clarity and focus. Act on your goals with confidence and courage. If you have been holding back, take this moment to show your strength, power and honour. Exercise your independence and align it with your family and community values.

ELEPHANT

> Keywords: wisdom, strength, family, gentleness, majesty, luck

The image of an elephant can mean different things to different people. It is a large, powerful animal that demands respect. Despite the elephant's size and strength, it has a gentle nature that makes it all the more lovable. It is known for its loyalty, immense emotional range and cultural-religious significance.

In Hinduism, the elephant is considered sacred. The deity Ganesha, known as the remover of obstacles, is associated with wisdom and new beginnings. Across all of Africa and Asia, elephants are featured in folklore, cultural practice and traditions, and associated with strength, power, wisdom, ancestral spirits, prosperity and royalty.

The elephant urges you to trust in your own wisdom and strength. Cherish your family and community and focus on building trust and loyalty in those relationships. You have a whole village ready to support you whenever that time may come. The elephant appears to remind you of the importance of protecting that. If you are facing adversity, know that you won't need to do it alone.

Elk

Keywords: stamina, strength, survival, endurance, grounding

The elk is a symbol of sovereignty. When it appears to you, it does so to bless you with strength and endurance to face whatever challenges may come your way. Take the reins of destiny and steer them in your own chosen direction. Have courage to push forward into your own path, simultaneously demonstrating for others what they can do for themselves. You're not only sovereign, but also a leader. Honour your wisdom and you will not just survive, but thrive.

Fox

Keywords: trickery, cunning, stealth, adaptability, playful, discerning

The fox is known for its cleverness and adaptability. When the fox appears to you, it's a sign that you must embrace your own cunning nature and trust your instincts. Be discerning about the people around you, but not at the expense of the joy and fun you have in your life. Blend into your surroundings like the stealthy fox, doing the work quietly so as not to be interrupted or distracted, knowing you'll have your chance to shine and play in due time.

Frog

Keywords: metamorphosis, fertility, birth, rebirth, luck

The frog appears as a symbol of transformation and renewal. Its enormous metamorphosis from tadpole to frog serves as a lesson for you to embrace change, knowing you will come out of it stronger and more capable – a whole new you. When the frog appears, you're being asked to reflect on the past so you may release all that does not serve you. This cleansing of mind, body and spirit makes space for new energy to come through, welcoming new beginnings – a rebirthing. When the frog appears, know that luck is on your side.

Grasshopper

Keywords: opportunities, faith, prosperity, luck

The grasshopper encourages you to take a leap of faith. Prosperity is on the horizon, so be patient and know that luck is on your side. When the grasshopper appears, you're reminded to embrace opportunities with open arms.

Hawk

Keywords: focus, intuition, clarity, insight, spiritual guidance

Trust in your vision, observe your surroundings and adapt as necessary. When the hawk appears, you're asked to embrace your role as a guardian. Protect those under your care and watch over them carefully.

Horse

Keywords: freedom, strength, adventure, wild spirit

The horse asks you to embrace your freedom! Move through life with grace and strength. Now is the time to seize the opportunity for adventure. Welcome new opportunities with an open heart.

Hummingbird

Keywords: joy, agility, speed, healing, beauty

When the hummingbird appears, you're asked to embrace gratitude for even the smallest of blessings and appreciate the power these blessings have to change your life, bringing you meaning and purpose. Look for joy in your life, and you will feel the heaviness dissipate. Maintain a positive attitude and remember the beauty that surrounds you.

Jaguar

Keywords: strength, stealth, mystery, power, courage

The jaguar invites you to lean into your power and trust your instincts. Have courage if you have challenges ahead, and trust that you will overcome them if you act with grace and strength. The jaguar appears when you are required to act independently, diligently and fearlessly.

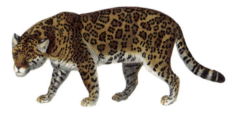

Kangaroo

Keywords: strength, endurance, adaptability, protection

The kangaroo encourages you to find balance in your life. Protect those you love and note the importance of family bonds. Just as the kangaroo protects its young joey, you must put your energy towards protecting your child or someone vulnerable who is in your care right now. The kangaroo asks you to be adaptable and to push through the discomfort of challenges.

Koala

Keywords: nurturing, family, peace, comfort, calm

The koala appears to you as a reminder to cherish your family and community. You must embrace the nurturer within, care for those who are vulnerable, and comfort those in need. In some ways, the koala asks you to be a protector. Known for its slow pace and gentle nature, the koala encourages you to foster a peaceful and relaxing environment for yourself and your family at this time.

Lion

Keywords: power, dominance, leadership, courage, strength, responsibility

The lion, with its demanding presence, is majestic and powerful. Associated with pride, strength and authority, it dominates the jungle at the top of the food chain. When the lion appears to you, you are asked to tap into your inner courage and lead with confidence. Now is your time to stand tall, with pride and dignity. Don't let others step over you. You must trust your strength and leadership capabilities, and use them to stand up for what you believe in. You have the responsibility to protect your pride.

Luna moth

Keywords: connection to the moon, inner peace, insight, transformation, spiritual connection

The lunar moth is associated with the transformation and phases of the moon. Move with the cycles of the moon, and allow your inner voice to guide you through these phases. Now is the time to embrace change, and see it as an opportunity for growth. Resisting change will only take away your peace.

Mantis

Keywords: meditation, patience, mindfulness, discernment, stillness

Practise patience and stillness. The mantis appears to tell you to focus on your goals and to be mindful every step along the way. Now is a time to embrace meditation, quiet time and privacy.

Mouse

Keywords: resourcefulness, skill, modesty, not to be underestimated

The mouse encourages you to be resourceful. Pay close attention to all the finer details and approach situations with caution. People may be underestimating you at this time and you can use that to your advantage, but do it modestly and carefully. The mouse has appeared to ask you to be diligent.

Owl

Keywords: wisdom, spiritual messenger, intuition, insight

The owl is known for its nocturnal nature and mystery. Its unusual ability to rotate its head almost 300 degrees, combined with its keen eyesight and sharp hearing, makes it an exceptional hunter. This bird of prey has long been shrouded in speculation, folklore and myth. The owl has the ability to camouflage its body, allowing it to blend in with leaves, twigs and branches, helping it stay undetected from predators.

The owl asks you to explore the depths of your intuition and trust your inner wisdom to guide you to uncovered truths. Take time to connect with your innate knowing and the psychic power buried within. When the owl appears, you're encouraged to metaphorically open your eyes and listen carefully. There is much to be uncovered. The owl often appears during times of transition, to guide you through the astral plane, and to help you reach understanding and connect with your unique magical power.

Panther

Keywords: power, grace, strength, protection, feminine, rebirth

The panther appears during trying times, when courage and strength are required. You're encouraged to stride forward with confidence and grace. When the panther appears, it asks you to be determined, nurture your needs and transform, if you must, in order to protect yourself and all that you have worked hard to build.

Peacock

Keywords: beauty, grace, confidence, glamour, integrity, attraction

The peacock encourages you to embrace your beauty and confidence. Take pride in your achievements and don't be afraid to stand out. Now is a time for self-assuredness. When the peacock appears, you're asked to pursue your visions and potential with integrity and allow your work to dazzle. Don't dim your creativity: embrace it, expand it. Now is the time to shine.

Platypus

Keywords: curiosity, playfulness, creativity

The platypus's message is to embrace your unique gifts and celebrate what makes you special. You must follow your curiosity and allow it to unveil new experiences and approaches to life. There is so much creative potential within you, and when the platypus appears you're asked to recognise and utilise this gift.

Rabbit

Keywords: fertility, abundance, sensitivity, gentleness, renewal

The rabbit appears as a messenger of fruition, fertility and abundance. Allow your life to follow the path towards a new beginning. You're being asked to lean into the process and make room for space to grow. When the rabbit appears, the message is that now is the time for renewal.

Rat

Keywords: adaptability, survival, intelligence, overcoming obstacles

The rat encourages you to trust your instincts and be resourceful. Use your intelligence to overcome any obstacles. Now is the time for survival, and you must adapt to your circumstances to get through the current challenges you face.

A rat can also appear as a warning that there is a 'rat' amongst you. When the rat appears as a bad omen, you're warned there may be sneakiness, deception, betrayal or bad luck surrounding you. You must urgently cleanse this energy.

172 ✦ *A practical guide to* **MAGIC IN NATURE**

RAVEN

> Keywords: magic, prophecy, wisdom, subconscious, rebirth, transformation

The raven is a creature that evokes fear and adoration, depending on who you ask. It is known for its intelligence and social behaviour, glossy black feathers, large beak and robust build. It is a powerful bird, both physically and in its spiritual meaning.

The raven acts as a messenger between the physical world and the magical world. It has been associated with death and rebirth through many spiritual traditions worldwide. If you would like to work with the energy of the raven, it can be invoked in rituals relating to shadow work, transformation and psychic development. You might also turn to the raven to seek wisdom or guidance on your spiritual path.

The raven encourages you to explore your subconscious. Trust in your intuitive abilities and gifts. Now is a good time to work with your shadow self and seek deeper understanding. When the raven appears, you're warned that transformation is on its way, and you may experience profound change or even a rebirth of sorts. Because of the deep association with death, the raven is sometimes seen as a bad omen, warning of ill fortune.

ANIMALS ÷ 173

Serpent

Keywords: healing, rebirth, transformation, divine feminine, sensuality, wisdom

The serpent, or snake, asks you to embrace transformation and healing. Symbolising rebirth, it sheds its skin as it grows, much like you shed layers of yourself as you grow on your journey in life. The snake represents healing and wisdom, and is often associated with kundalini energy – the life force that energises our entire being. Its association with the cyclical nature of life links it to renewal and change. The snake carries sacred knowledge and imparts that knowledge when it appears to you. When the serpent appears to you, you're asked to welcome personal transformation and seek deeper understanding by shedding the layers of old habits and beliefs to make space for rebirth.

Shark

Keywords: survival, determination, strength, power, domination, instinct

The shark is an animal that evokes fear in most, due to its sheer power, strength and intensity. When it appears to you, you're encouraged to harness your own power and intensity, and use your survival instincts to navigate your current situation. The shark asks you to protect yourself and have determination. Now is a time to tap into your primal nature and focus on getting yourself through this period until you have reached safety and stability.

Spider

Keywords: creativity, manifesting, patience, connection, wisdom, luck

The spider encourages you to embrace your creativity and patience. Like the spider weaves its web with care and craftsmanship, you must weave a life for yourself and manifest what you want to create for yourself in the future. When the spider appears, you're reminded of the interconnectedness of all things and that you must focus on creating balance.

Stag

Keywords: leadership, fertility, renewal, protection

The stag appears as a messenger of strength and sovereignty. When it appears you're reminded of the importance of protecting your dear ones and leading with grace. Trust

174 ÷ *A practical guide to* **MAGIC IN NATURE**

that you have what it takes to lead, and know that your leadership skills will carry you and your community to a renewed place of strength and harmony.

Swan

Keywords: grace, beauty, love, partnership, balance, innocence, purification

The swan encourages you to embrace beauty and grace. Now is a time for love and serenity. Nurture your romantic relationships. When the swan appears, you're asked to find balance in your life, open your heart, and trust that the love you're receiving is pure and true.

Tiger

Keywords: power, strength, dominance, wards off evil spirits

The tiger asks you to embrace your power and passion. You must maintain your independence, confidence and strength at this time. When the tiger appears, you're reminded to pursue your goals with determination. The tiger is a dominant creature, asking you to evaluate how you can dominate in an area of your life, not as a way of causing harm to others but as a way of protecting yourself and your own needs. Call upon the tiger to ward off evil spirits when you feel that your energy is being interfered with.

Toad

Keywords: breaking hexes, cleansing, protection, transformation

The toad is a creature of transformation and adaptability. It undergoes a cycle from egg,

ANIMALS ✣ 175

to tadpole, to mature toad. This metamorphosis is a message to you that change is on the way and that you will be stronger because of it. The toad appears to remind you there is potential for growth now. Along with its messages of strength and transformation, the toad also brings messages of protection and cleansing. Call upon the toad when you need to cleanse, break a hex, or otherwise rid yourself or your home from unwanted energies.

Turtle

Keywords: longevity, protection, stability, inward reflection

The turtle brings a message of patience and longevity. You are asked to trust that with wisdom and endurance, you can navigate anything life throws at you and find stability for yourself. Like the hard shell that protects the turtle from predators, you're encouraged to protect and shield yourself at this time. Take time to look inwards and reconnect with yourself.

Unicorn

Keywords: magic, purity, guidance, wonder

The unicorn is a powerful magical creatures known for its purity, majesty and gentleness. The unicorn encourages you to embrace your own pure nature, innate magic and beauty. It guides you through inspiration and wonder. When the unicorn appears before you, you're being called to connect with a higher power and to believe in the impossible.

Wasp

Keywords: productivity, assertiveness, contracts, planning, business

The wasp asks you to embrace productivity and teamwork. Now is a time for finalising contracts, planning and organising business decisions. If you have been avoiding paperwork or hesitating on any business ideas, now is the time to take action. When the wasp appears, you're asked to maintain order and structure in your life.

Whale

Keywords: ancient wisdom, sacredness, spiritual growth, communication, emotions

The whale is a majestic creature that carries ancient wisdom. It asks you to dive deep within yourself and to trust your own inner wisdom. The whale encourages you to express yourself and open up to communicate openly, from your heart. Dive deep into your emotions and honour them. Now is the time to process and heal these deep emotions, rather than to drown in them. When the whale appears, you're asked to open up to spiritual growth and make space in your life for exploring your inner world and the ancient, magical knowledge of the world around you.

Wolf

Keywords: loyalty, teamwork, community, instinct, independence

The wolf symbolises intuition, freedom and powerful social bonds. It encourages you to trust your instincts and embrace your inner strength. Find a balance between your independence and social responsibility. Loyalty is an important quality, and there is strength in a loyal community. When the wolf appears, you're encouraged to be a good team member, whether that's in the context of family, partnerships, business or sport. Be reliable and dependable while also making time to work on yourself on a personal level.

ANIMALS ✢ 177

ANIMALS ASSOCIATED WITH EARTH

ANIMALS ASSOCIATED WITH WIND

——— ANIMALS ASSOCIATED WITH WATER ———

——— ANIMALS ASSOCIATED WITH FIRE ———

PART 4:

CELESTIAL BODIES

INTRODUCTION TO THE PLANETS AND STARS

Many cycles can be experienced and witnessed in the natural world, all of which bring their unique magic into your life. This section of the book explores the magic of planets and celestial bodies, from the earth's cycles reflected in the changing seasons, to the unique power of the days of the week and the magic governed by celestial bodies. Each planet has its distinct vibrations and attributes that influence our actions and intentions.

Throughout the history of ceremonial magic, planetary influences and hours have held significant importance. Historically significant grimoires, such as the The Key of Solomon, highlight the distinct powers of specific planetary alignment. For example, 'the days and hours of Jupiter' are believed to help with 'obtaining honours, acquiring riches, contracting friendships, preserving health', according to the 16th-century text. By understanding these forces, you can harness their power to enhance your daily life and deepen your magical practice.

HOW TO READ THE CELESTIAL BODY PROFILES

Each celestial body profile is structured to provide information that is relevant to that particular planet.

Day

Each day of the week is ruled by a celestial body, offering an advantage for planning rituals, casting spells or practising magic. By aligning your work with the celestial body governing each day, you can amplify the effectiveness of your practices and harness the day's specific metaphysical properties.

Days of the week

Monday: intuition, divination, fertility, emotions, dreams and protection

Tuesday: victory, courage, strength, vitality, courage, conflicts

Wednesday: learning, communication, travel, money, divination

Thursday: justice, luck, prosperity, expansion, growth, abundance

Friday: romance, love, friendship, creativity, beauty, pleasure

Saturday: transformation, protection, banishing, cleansing, discipline, stability

Sunday: abundance, success, leadership, joy, vitality

Colour

The colour associated with a celestial body does not refer to its literal colour but rather the colour that aligns with the energy and magical properties it represents. Enhance the power of your rituals and attract desired energy by integrating the colours associated with that celestial body.

Element

The term 'element' denotes one of the four fundamental elements: wind, water, earth or fire. Understanding the element linked to a celestial body is helpful as these profoundly influence the energy of the planet. To enhance the power of your rituals or magical work, include other items associated with that element.

For example: if working with the element of water, you could perform your ritual by the ocean, place a bowl of water on your altar, make a tea to sip during the ritual or incorporate bathing into your ritual.

Metal

Infusing your magical tools, talismans or rituals with metals aligns your work with distinct planetary energies, influencing the results to reflect the unique properties linked to each celestial body.

Zodiac

Each zodiac sign has a governing planet that influences the energy of the people who are born under that planet. Learning the ruling planets of zodiac signs can help you better understand yourself and others.

Angels and gods

Each celestial body is connected to various gods and angels. You can work with angels or invoke gods, either through rituals, prayers or offerings. These are ways to honour and establish a connection with these divine entities. This practice includes calling upon the energies of the deity for a specific purpose or spiritual experience.

Plants

Fruits, herbs, spices, flowers and various other plants are energetically linked to specific celestial bodies. While in ritual, during spell work, kitchen witchery or similar practices involving these plants, you can refer to this guide to discover additional plants ruled by the same planet. By incorporating these plants into your recipes and focusing in on complementary plant energies, you can enhance the potency of your magic.

Crystals

Much like plants, crystals are energetically linked to specific celestial bodies. By working with these crystals you can incorporate the associated energies of both the crystals and also the celestial body that rules that crystal.

Organs

Claudius Ptolemy (c. 100–170 CE), a Greek-Roman astronomer, discovered that the planets are associated with various aspects of human life. He assigned specific characteristics and qualities to each planet, connecting them to aspects of the natural world and human experience. The organs listed in this entry indicated the organ associated with that particular planet. This provides insight into how ancient cultures sought to understand the intricate connections between celestial forces and human well-being.

Chakras

The energy centres in our bodies are governed by the planets. By understanding the relationship between each chakra and its governing planet or celestial body, you can use this information to enhance your spiritual practice, recognise patterns from your birth chart and work with the energies more intentionally. This connection between the planets and your body demonstrates the way that you are a reflection of the magical cycles in nature and that everything is intrinsically connected.

THE
CELESTIAL
BODIES

———

Our solar system

Mercury

Day: Wednesday

Colour: orange

Element: wind

Metal: Mercury

Zodiac: Gemini, Virgo

Angels and gods: Hermes, Thoth, Odin

Plants: dill, lemongrass, marjoram, mint, parsley, echinacea, lavender, lily of the valley, fennel, mulberry, pomegranate, mandrake, pistachio, almond

Crystals: lapis lazuli, blue calcite, fluorite, kyanite

Organs: nervous system, brain, respiratory system

Chakra: throat

Mercury is linked to communication, intellect and creativity. It is used for rituals involving writing, communication skills and gaining knowledge. Mercury governs how we think, learn and process information. It influences our problem solving, brainstorming and all areas of mental focus.

Venus

Day: Friday

Colour: green

Element: water

Metal: copper

Zodiac: Libra, Taurus

Angels and gods: Anael, Inanna, Venus, Aphrodite

Plants: caper, sorrel, grains, thyme, catmint, cornflower. daffodil, elderflower, feverfew, foxglove, heather, hibiscus, mugwort, orchid, rose, vervain, violet, yarrow, apple, apricot, avocado, banana, cherry, corn, licorice, peach, pear, persimmon, raspberry, strawberry, tomato, vanilla

Crystals: rose quartz, kunzite, emerald, pink tourmaline

Organs: reproductive system, lymphatic system

Chakra: heart

Venus is linked to love, indulgence, and harmony. It is used in rituals involving romantic relationships, self-love, and artistic endeavours. Venus governs our connection with others, appreciation for beauty and our romantic inclinations. The position of Venus in your birth chart reveals your relationship needs, preferences in a partner and your attitude towards pleasure.

CELESTIAL BODIES ☦ 189

EARTH

SUMMER
Summer is marked by long, bright sun-filled days. It is a time for celebration, relaxation and vitality. With a zest for life, summer brings opportunity for aspirations and goals to be realised.

AUTUMN
Autumn brings cooling temperatures and falling leaves. It is a time of harvest to prepare for the rest and dormancy of winter. The fruits of our labour are now showing after the groundwork has been laid. In autumn we release what no longer serves us to prepare for the renewal cycle ahead.

WINTER
Winter is a time for introspection, rest and renewal. Life slows down and we turn inwards to reflect. It is during winter that we do the inner work and prepare for the rebirth and growth that is due to arrive in spring.

SPRING
Spring is a time of awakening after a dormant period. It marks new beginnings as nature bursts with life, plants and fruits growing in abundance. Spring inspires positivity, optimism and taking action on a fresh start or a new opportunity.

Mars

Day: Tuesday

Colour: red

Element: fire

Metal: iron

Zodiac: Aries

Angels and gods: Ares, Mars

Plants: allspice, basil, chilli, coriander, cumin, pepper, tobacco, wormwood, garlic, ginger, onion, dragon's blood, stinging nettle, milk thistle, hawthorn, holly, pine

Crystals: carnelian, fire agate, tiger eye, rhodochrosite, malachite

Organs: adrenaline, sexual organs, muscles

Chakra: root

Mars is associated with courage, protection and aggression. It is used in rituals related to conflict resolution, strength, and defence. Mars governs our drive, ambitions and competitive instincts. It drives us to pursue our goals and how or when we take action to achieve them.

Jupiter

Day: Thursday

Colour: blue

Element: fire

Metal: tin

Zodiac: Sagittarius

Angels and gods: Zeus, Thor, Indra

Plants: agrimony, anise, bloody dock, clove, nutmeg, oak, sage, hyssop, carnation, star anise, dandelion, honeysuckle, fig, chestnut, banksia, maple, wood betony

Crystals: citrine, fire agate, pyrite, aventurine, rutile

Organs: liver, pancreas

Chakra: third eye

Jupiter is associated with growth, abundance and expansion. Working with Jupiter is useful for rituals related to wealth, prosperity, and spiritual development. Jupiter governs our luck, optimism and pursuits of deeper philosophical learning, driving us to seek new experiences. The placement of Jupiter in your birth chart can indicate what areas of your life will be blessed, where you will gain your sense of purpose and how to approach challenges in life.

Saturn

Day: Saturday

Colour: black

Element: earth

Metal: lead

Zodiac: Capricorn

Angels and gods: Tzaphqiel, Cronus

Plants: belladonna, wolfsbane, mullein, beetroot, beech, cyprus, elm

Crystals: black tourmaline, obsidian, smoky quartz, bloodstone

Organs: skeletal system, bones, teeth, skin

Chakra: crown

Saturn is associated with discipline, limitation and protection. It is useful to work with Saturn during rituals related to banishing negativity, breaking bad habits and building endurance. Saturn drives us to work hard, build resilience and confront any limitations we are challenged with. Saturn's placement in your birth chart highlights areas where you will be challenged in facing fears and building secure foundations for long-term success.

Uranus*

Zodiac: Aquarius

Crystals: labradorite, lapis lazuli, cavansite

Organ: electromagnetic system

Uranus is associated with innovation, change and individualism. It rules over unconventional thinking, rebellion and revolutionary ideas, facilitating breakthroughs in freedom, independence and embracing your unique self.

Neptune*

Zodiac: Pisces

Angels and gods: Poseidon, Neptune

Crystals: amethyst, azurite, kyanite

Organs: pineal gland, endocrine system

Neptune is associated with dreams, intuition, imagination and spirituality. It governs your subconscious mind, aiding in creativity and transcendence, but can also hinder with confusion and delusion.

Pluto*

Zodiac: Scorpio

Angels and gods: Hades

Crystals: moonstone, obsidian, rhodonite, carnelian

Organs: DNA, cells

Pluto is associated with transformation and the depths of your psyche. It rules over psychological evolution, control and power dynamics, and confronting intense experiences.

*Uranus, Neptune and Pluto

These planets are less understood. Their astrological interpretations are relatively recent developments in modern astrology in comparison to the other planets, which have a long history in traditional astrology.

CELESTIAL BODIES ✦ 193

SUN

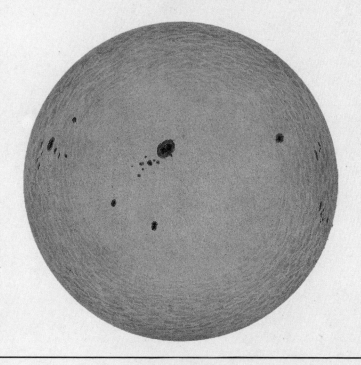

Day: Sunday
Colour: Yellow
Element: fire
Metal: gold
Zodiac: Leo
Angels and gods: Apollo, Ra, Helios, Surya
Plants: bay laurel, calendula, chamomile, cinnamon, juniper, rosemary, St John's wort, saffron, marigold, sunflower
Crystals: sunstone, citrine, tiger eye, pyrite
Organs: heart, immune system
Chakra: sun

The sun is associated with success, power, authority and healing. It is often invoked for rituals related to personal growth, achievement, and vitality. The sun represents the essence of our being, identity and life force. The sun in your birth chart represents your primary motivations in life, your ego and the central aspects that your life revolves around.

Beyond astrology, in new age philosophy and across many spiritual practices the sun is a symbol of life. It brings vitality, divine light and healing. Through the energy and life force of the sun's divine light, all of life is interconnected. It's for this reason that throughout history and across all cultures, either the sun or sun deities have been worshipped. Some examples include Ra (Egyptian mythology), Helios (Greek mythology) and Apollo (Greek mythology).

In ritual or ceremony, the sun is often honoured to invoke blessings, growth and abundance. Visualisation of the sun can bring energy, clarity and expansion of consciousness. Gold or talismans made to symbolise the sun can be used on your altar to invoke the powerful solar energy. Sunlight has healing properties that promote overall well-being and is vital for healthy functioning of your physical, emotional and spiritual bodies.

MOON

Day: Monday
Colour: white
Element: water
Metal: silver
Zodiac: Cancer
Angels and gods: Artemis, Selene, Luna, Chandra
Plants: eucalyptus, lemon balm, jasmine, lily, poppy, sacred lotus, blueberry, cabbage, cucumber, grape, lemon, potato, myrrh, coconut, aloe vera, willow
Crystals: pearl, larimar, moonstone, selenite, aquamarine
Organs: stomach, digestive system, fluids, breasts, female reproductive system, emotional body
Chakra: moon

The moon is a celestial body whose influence extends to all of the functions of the physical world, and into the spiritual and emotional realms of us humans.

When exploring the effects on us, the moon is associated with your emotions, intuition and subconscious mind. Working with the energy of the moon allows for the expansion of your imagination and subconscious exploration, which is essential for your personal growth and spiritual development.

We can look to the moon and observe its cycles, with its waxing and waning mirroring the phases we experience in our own lives. Our spiritual journeys often resemble a similar cycle of light and shadow, as we navigate the path towards spiritual fulfilment.

The moon also has significant influence on the plant world, and therefore significant influence over the healing properties when we explore the use of plants in herbalism.

Lunar-related plants have healing properties such as:

Cooling and soothing: e.g. cucumber, marshmallow root, chickweed
These plants are beneficial for calming and alleviating conditions associated with heat and inflammation.

Moisturising and nourishing: e.g. borage, fenugreek, violet
The moon is associated with water. Plants connected to the moon have moisturising and nourishing effects, making them suitable for conditions related to dryness or dehydration.

Emotional balance: e.g. chamomile, lavender, valerian
Lunar-related plants have a calming and emotionally balancing effect. They help with conditions related to mood swings or emotional regulation.

Purification and cleansing: e.g. cedar, frankincense, myrrh
The cyclical nature of the moon's phases is symbolic of the way in which lunar-related plants can be used for purification and cleansing, both physically and spiritually.

Psychic and intuitive enhancement: e.g. lemon balm, mugwort, star anise
These plants enhance psychic abilities, intuition, and dream work. They help you to connect with your subconscious mind.

Feminine health: e.g. chasteberry, raspberry leaf and yarrow
The moon's association with the feminine gives power to lunar-related plants when it comes to remedies for women's health issues, such as menstrual disorders and menopause.

CELESTIAL BODIES ÷ 197

MOON
PHASES
—

New moon

When the dark side of the moon is facing the earth, making it invisible. The new moon marks a time for new beginnings. It is a clean slate, creating an opportunity to plan ahead for the upcoming month and think about what you want to achieve or obtain.

Waxing crescent moon

When only a crescent of the moon is illuminated before the full moon. The waxing crescent moon is a time to set your intentions for the plans you made in the previous moon phase. Build momentum and focus your goals.

First quarter moon

Marks the transition between the waxing crescent moon and the waxing gibbous moon. The first quarter moon is the time to take practical action towards the intentions you are manifesting. Face any challenges that you have encountered head first, and breakthrough towards your goals.

Waxing gibbous moon

When the moon is more than half illuminated before the full moon. The waxing gibbous moon is a time to take stock of your success so far and refine any action you have taken to keep yourself on track. This moon phase is an opportunity to seek improvement.

Full moon

When the moon is completely illuminated. A full moon is an opportunity to connect with the divine. Enjoy the progress on your intentions that were set in the new moon phase and allow things to come to their natural completion. Reap the fruits of your labour.

Waning gibbous moon

When the moon is more than half illuminated after the full moon. The waning gibbous moon is a time in the cycle to slow down and observe. Have gratitude for what was accomplished. Now is a time to turn inwards and accept the end of the cycle and prepare for the release that is to come in the next moon phase.

Third quarter moon

Marks the transition between the waning gibbous moon and the waning crescent moon. The third quarter moon is a time to release. Let go of anything that no longer serves you. Weed out bad habits and unfulfilling or harmful commitments and cleanse yourself and your space.

Waning crescent moon

When only a crescent of the moon is illuminated after the full moon. Take some time to rest and resct. Rest is a natural part of every cycle, and sometimes the hardest. Surrender to the stillness and know that you will have lots of work to do when the new moon returns.

Special moon phases

Blood moon: a total lunar eclipse, where the earth is positioned between the sun and moon, casting a shadow on the moon. During the blood moon, the moon will illuminate red. The blood moon brings the opportunity for rebirth and change. It highlights the aspects of ourselves that we keep hidden in the shadows. Emotions such as grief, anger and jealousy may be heightened at this time. By bringing our shadow to the surface, the blood moon offers us a chance for introspection and growth.

Blue moon: when a second full moon occurs within one calendar month. The blue moon is a rare and special moon phase that offers heightened clarity and connection to your spiritual self. It is considered to be a time of luck and blessings, heightening your opportunities for manifesting and connecting with the divine.

Supermoon: when the full moon coincides with the moon during its stage when it is closest to earth in its orbit. This moon appears larger and brighter than a normal full moon. There are usually only three or four supermoons per year. The heightened energy of the supermoon amplifies your intentions and increases the potency of any magical workings. It is a powerful time for recharging; however, it can also bring energetic and emotional overwhelm to many. It is important to remain centred and grounded during the supermoon. The energies amplified during this time can vary depending on the astrological season that the supermoon falls under.

Super blood moon: a rare occasion when a supermoon occurs at the same time as a lunar eclipse, causing the moon to illuminate red. The super blood moon brings combined and intensified powers of both a blood moon and a supermoon. It can be a time of significant change and transformation, as well as overwhelm and instability.

Black moon: when a second new moon occurs within one calendar month. The black moon is a second opportunity within that one-month period for new beginnings and setting intentions or starting new projects.

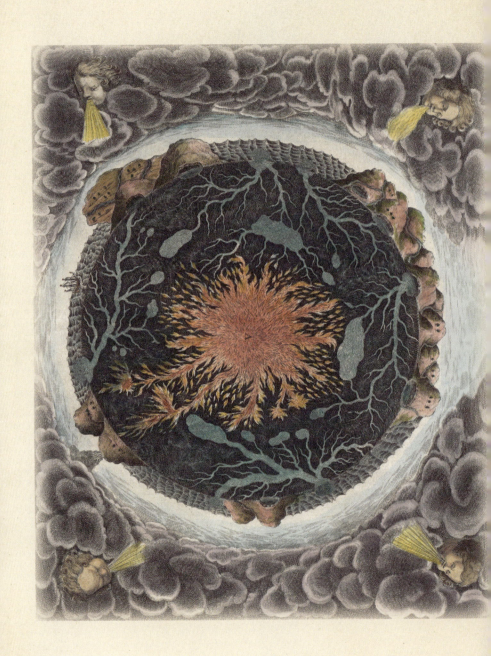

PART 5:

THE ELEMENTS

INTRODUCTION TO THE ELEMENTS

Understanding the magic of the elements helps us to harness those energies in our everyday life and in our magical workings. Each element possesses unique qualities that can be integrated into your spiritual practice, and utilising these principles can enhance your rituals, meditation and healing.

If you choose to keep an altar at home, a place where you will conduct all of your magical workings, having all of the elements represented on your altar can enhance the power of your spells and rituals. Some examples of items you can use to represent the elements on your altar are:

- earth: soil, salt, plants, crystals, herbs, wood
- wind: feathers, incense, bird or butterfly totems, fan
- fire: candles, ash, incense, pyramid
- water: shells, bowl of water, perfumes and oils, chalice.

For a full list of crystals or herbs and their associated elements, refer to the previous sections on crystals and plant magic.

As you explore the magic in nature, pay as much attention to the magic in the invisible natural forces around you as you do the natural objects and creatures such as crystals, herbs, animals and the like. You can harness this elemental magic in your spiritual practice, or simply notice and appreciate the way that the elements influence your day-to-day life. Do you notice how secure you feel when you sit in nature, the emotional release you feel when you spend time by natural waters, how inspired you feel when you are seated around a bonfire, or how invigorating it feels when you walk through the city on a windy day? Embrace the elements and let their magic enhance your spiritual workings, bringing you closer to nature and to integrating the mysteries and the magic hidden in nature.

THE ELEMENTS ÷ 205

WORKING WITH THE ELEMENTS

Earth

Earth is the element of grounding, physicality and what is tangible in this existence. It is connected to health, materialism and stability.

The earth element is associated with the direction of the north, symbolising strength, security and resilience.

In magical practice, earth helps you to cultivate stability in your life, is useful in grounding rituals, enhances your health and empowers you to manifest your goals. Earth's energy is supportive and nurturing, making it useful in rituals or spells related to healing or for gaining material wealth.

Connecting with earth

- Stand on the earth, barefoot.

- Visualise roots extending from your body into the earth.

- Incorporate earth element tools into your practice, such as wood, plants or soil.

- Work with earth element herbs or crystals.

Associations with earth

Tarot symbol: pentacles

Zodiac signs: Capricorn, Virgo, Taurus

Colour: green

Season: winter

Chakra: root

Wind (air)

Wind, also referred to as air, is the element of the mind and intellect. It governs our thoughts, communication and imagination. When you work with the power of wind, you connect to the realms of inspiration and insight.

The wind element is associated with the direction of the east, where the sun rises and symbolises new beginnings, clarity and focus.

In magical practices, wind is used to aid mental clarity, creativity and mental agility. It is useful in spells or rituals that require brainstorming, writing or expressing ideas. It is also useful to call upon the power of wind during meditation to clear away any brain fog or mental noise, and to open opportunities for higher knowing and deepened intuition.

Connecting with wind

- Meditate in open space where there is a breeze.
- Visualise the wind sweeping away mental clutter.
- Incorporate wind element tools into your practice, such as feathers, incense or wind chimes.
- Work with wind element herbs or crystals.

Associations with wind

Tarot symbol: swords

Zodiac signs: Gemini, Libra, Aquarius

Colour: yellow

Season: spring

Chakra: third eye, throat

Water

Water is the element of the subconscious. It is connected to your feelings, emotions, and intuition.

The water element is associated with the west, symbolic of the setting sun and introspection.

In magical practice, water is essential for emotional healing, enhancing psychic abilities and facilitating deep introspection. It helps you to flow with life's changes and connect to your inner self. Water rituals can cleanse emotional blockages and enhance your psychic gifts.

Connecting with water

- Spend time near lakes, rivers or the ocean.
- Incorporate water element tools into your practice, such as a chalice, seashells, mirrors or water.
- Visualise yourself surrounded by peaceful, flowing water.
- Work with water element crystals and herbs.

Associations with water

Tarot symbol: cups

Zodiac signs: Cancer, Pisces, Scorpio

Colour: blue

Season: autumn

Chakra: heart, sacral

Fire

Fire is the element of transformation and action. It is connected to your passion, creativity, and ambition.

The fire element is associated with the direction of the south, symbolising the midday sun, the height of energy and vitality.

In magical practice, fire is used to harness inspiration, motivation and the pursuit of goals. It is useful in spells or rituals related to change, transformation, protection or creativity. Fire has a transformative power that burns away the old, making way for the new.

Connecting with fire

- Try hot yoga.
- Integrate candles or fire into your magical workings.
- Meditate under the sun.
- Visualise a fire burning from within you, growing stronger with every breath.
- Work with fire element herbs and crystals.

Associations with fire

Tarot symbol: wands

Zodiac signs: Aries, Leo, Sagittarius

Colour: red

Season: summer

Chakra: solar plexus

PART 6

THE MAGIC
IN YOU

INTRODUCTION TO YOUR PERSONAL MAGIC

You are an integral part of the natural world, not separate from it. You, like nature, possess unique and powerful magic and wonder.

Nature serves as a boundless source of inspiration. Whether it's the roaring ocean that demands our respect or the subtlety of a starry night filling us with awe, nature's beauty and complexity cannot be overstated.

Recognising the magic in nature is a step towards understanding your own magic. Just as the universe is a vast cosmos of stardust, water, carbon and more, you too are composed of these same fundamental elements. This is a kind of cosmic kinship.

As above, so below,

As within, so without.

Beyond your physical make-up, it's the natural rhythms, such as the moon's pull on tides or the sun's nurturing rays, that reveal an intricate mirroring between you and the world. You are not just an observer, but a perfectly placed element in the natural rhythms of the world, experiencing your own cycles. As the seasons change, so do our moons and nutritional needs. As we age, we experience physical, emotional and hormonal changes to our bodies; some of us experience menstrual cycles; every single one of us witnesses and eventually experiences the full cycle of life and death. A large part of our existence is in bearing witness to these many rhythms and cycles of life.

Just as flowers bloom and humbly grace the world with their presence, we, too, contribute to the enchantment of our surroundings by simply being. Embracing this concept, we recognise the inherent value of our existence, not defined by

THE MAGIC IN YOU ✦ **213**

achievements but by the enchantment we bring into the world. Whether you purchased this book to aid you as you perform rituals, or simply wished to explore all the ways that magic manifests in the world, either way, it does not change that you are enchanted. A human who never intentionally participates in magic, and a person who dedicates their entire life to magic, are both filled with magic by simply being. Our existence is a testament to the magic of life itself. Just as nature is powerful and magical, so are you. By embracing our natural connection to the world, we can learn to appreciate the beauty in our simple existence and find solace in the enchantment that surrounds us.

You are a miracle.

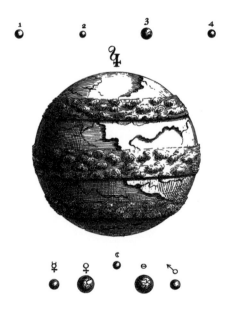

CLEARING YOUR ENERGY

It's important to practise good energetic hygiene. Just as we clean our physical bodies and our homes, it's also important to energetically cleanse ourselves. By maintaining a cleansed energetic field, you are also ensuring you maintain your magical power, and that you can practise your spiritual or magical rituals and ceremonies without the interference of outside forces. Energetic cleansing is also an important part of ensuring psychic protection.

How to clear your energy

Candles: light a white candle while setting a clear intention for cleansing your energy field.

Visualisation meditation: close your eyes and visualise a large ball of divine light above you. Slowly, focus the ball of light to move around your body and, as it does, washing away any doubts, fears, stagnant or negative energies. Take your time to move through all areas of your body and then allow the ball of light to grow larger and larger in size until it completely encapsulates you. Hold this position for as long as you feel comfortable. Your energy is now cleared.

Smoke cleansing: make a custom incense blend using herbs for protection, purification and blessing. As you burn them, use the smoke to cleanse yourself and your space, ensuring you keep a pure energetic atmosphere. A powerful blend to try is frankincense, myrrh, dried lavender and dried rosemary.

Grounding: stand outdoors with your bare feet on the earth, or sit at the base of a tree. Close your eyes and take deep, slow intentional breaths. By doing this you will resync to the earth's natural rhythms. Allow any unwanted energies to travel through your body and into the earth to be transmuted. Allow

THE MAGIC IN YOU ✦ 215

your body to welcome any grounded, supportive energy being offered by the earth, and your skin to absorb vital energy through the sunlight bathing you. Do this exercise for at least 10 minutes.

Crystal body grid: lay somewhere comfortable and place black tourmaline, selenite, smoky quartz and rose quartz crystals around you, wherever you intuitively feel they should be placed. Allow the crystal energy to cleanse, purify and bring divine white light and loving energy into your auric field. There are many crystals you can use for cleansing your energy – the suggested crystals above are a great starting point if you're inexperienced with crystals.

Ritual bath: use a combination of salts and cleansing herbs to draw yourself a cleansing bath. As you immerse yourself in the water, visualise your body being energetically cleansed by the water, herbs and salts.

USING TOOLS

Using tools such as crystals, candles, herbs and so on enhances your magic by helping you to focus your intention. Tools allow you to apply your magic in a way that amplifies it by combining your intentions with items that share corresponding energies. These items can then act as an extension of your will, channelling your energy and manipulating where it is directed, as well as enhancing your power, which helps to preserve your energy.

Pendulums

Pendulums are powerful tools for energy cleansing and gaining insight. Choose a pendulum that you feel strongly connected to, to ensure that your energy is aligned with the tool. Always cleanse before use. Sit comfortably with your pendulum and hold it at the end of the chain, allowing it to hang freely. Set your intention, whether it's to clear your energy or to gain insight; ask the pendulum to show you a 'yes' response. Observe its movements, and then follow up by asking it to show you a 'no'. Use these movements to guide you in your pendulum session.

Candles

Before lighting your candle, take a moment to cleanse the space, hold your candle in your hands and set your intentions. Take a look at the magical correspondences of different coloured candles, so you can choose the right candle for your next ritual. When in doubt, work with a white candle and take extra care to focus your intention.

Candle colour correspondences

White – cleansing, purification, clarity, divine connection, healing

Black – protection, banishing, transmuting negativity

Brown – grounding, stability, home, family, security

Red – passion, courage, strength, grounding

Orange – joy, vitality, creativity, career, happiness

Yellow – confidence, intellect, memory, mental health

Green – abundance, prosperity, luck, money, fertility

Blue – communication, peace, intuition, healing

Purple – psychic power, meditation, wisdom, spiritual development

Pink – romance, friendship, emotional healing, harmony

CHAKRAS

Your chakras are energy centres within your body that influence your physical, emotional and spiritual well-being. Each chakra governs specific body parts and energetic needs or gifts. Teachings of the chakra system originate from ancient sacred Vedic texts from India. By learning about your chakras, you can better understand yourself, the magic within you, and how best to approach your physical, emotional and spiritual needs.

I have provided the unique associations of the seven primary chakras in this section including the specific days of the week, planetary influence, and an affirmation to help you attune that energy centre. Each chakra entry will explain the characteristics and significance of each chakra, offering insights on how to determine when your chakra is in alignment versus symptoms to look out for when the energy of that chakra is blocked. You will also find suggestions on how to recharge and balance your chakras when you have energy imbalances and blockages.

Crown – Sahasrara
Organ: pituitary gland, hair, brain
Day: Saturday
Planet: Saturn
Colour: white and purple
Affirmation: 'I am connected to the divine and open to receiving guidance'

The crown chakra is located at the top of the head. When the crown chakra is in alignment, it is the gateway to higher consciousness and spiritual connection. It represents our ability to be connected to the divine and transcend our physical limitations. When the energy is blocked we feel disconnected, confused and uncertain of our purpose in life.

Third eye – Ajna
Organ: pineal gland, eyes, ears, nose
Day: Thursday
Planet: Jupiter
Colour: indigo
Affirmation: 'I trust my intuition and inner wisdom'

The third-eye chakra is located between the brows. When the third eye is in alignment, it is associated with intuition, psychic power and spiritual awareness. It governs our ability to see beyond the physical realm. When the energy is blocked we struggle to discern intuition from anxieties, lack imagination and have trouble thinking clearly.

THE MAGIC IN YOU ⁑ 221

Throat – Vishuddha

Organ: thyroid gland, vocal cords, mouth, oesophagus
Day: Wednesday
Planet: Mercury
Colour: blue
Affirmation: 'I express my truth clearly and confidently'

The throat chakra is located within the throat. When the throat chakra is in alignment, it is the energy centre for communication, expression and truth. It enables us to express our thoughts and feelings authentically. When the energy is blocked we are afraid to speak, or we over-explain and interrupt others and struggle to articulate ourselves.

Heart – Anahata

Organ: thymus gland, heart, lung
Day: Friday
Planet: Venus
Colour: green and pink
Affirmation: 'I open my heart to love'

The heart chakra is in the centre of the chest. When the heart chakra is in alignment, it allows us to express love, compassion and empathy. It is the source of emotional healing and allows us to give and receive love freely. When the energy is blocked we have difficulty accepting love, aren't able to empathise with others, or hold on to emotions such as anger, grief, sadness and jealousy.

Solar plexus – Manipura

Organ: pancreas, liver, intestines, stomach, gallbladder
Day: Sunday
Planet: sun
Colour: yellow
Affirmation: 'I am confident and empowered'

The solar plexus chakra is located in the abdomen. When the solar plexus chakra is in alignment, we are filled with confidence and joy. It is the source of our self-esteem and motivation to thrive. When the energy is blocked, we have low self-esteem and feel insecure and unmotivated.

Sacral – Svadhisthana

Organ: adrenal glands, spleen, bladder, prostate, kidney
Day: Monday
Planet: moon
Colour: orange
Affirmation: 'I embrace pleasure and abundance'

The sacral chakra is located below the navel. When the sacral chakra is in alignment, we welcome pleasure, sexual freedom and emotional expression. The sacral chakra is the source of our creative energy and the centre from which we store our passions and manifesting power. When the energy is blocked we have creative blocks, feel shame and guilt, are afraid to make changes in our lives, feel that we don't deserve pleasure in life, and have trouble with intimacy.

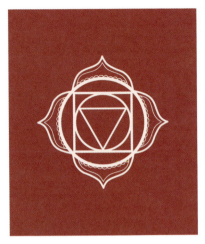

Root – Muladhara

Organ: reproductive glands
Day: Tuesday
Planet: Mars
Colour: red, brown, black
Affirmation: 'I am grounded and safe'

The root chakra is located at the base of the spine. When the root chakra is in alignment we feel grounded and secure, as if we have everything we need. It provides a sense of physical well-being, stability and connectedness. When the energy is blocked we feel unsafe, unstable, anxious and fearful.

How to balance and align your chakras

Balancing and aligning your chakras is an important step towards harmonising your mind, body and spirit. It aids an overall connection to self and improves well-being. The way in which you approach balancing your chakras can be simple and integrated into your day-to-day lifestyle, or complex and ceremonial in nature. Do whichever approach appeals to you and trust in your inner knowing of what works best for your own needs. Here are some suggestions for different ways that you can achieve this balance.

Affirmations

Affirmations are powerful statements that can help to align your chakras for focusing your intentions. Use the affirmations provided above to reinforce the vibrational frequency of the statement and energetically integrate it. Repeating these affirmations can be a daily exercise or something that is done when you intuitively feel that an energetic realignment is needed.

Yoga

Yoga can balance your energy centres through physical movement. Specific yoga poses will target different chakras. Therefore, a dedicated yoga practice can help to maintain a healthy, aligned energetic body.

Diet

Your diet plays a crucial role in your energetic health. By eating foods that correspond with the colours of each chakra, you ensure that you meet your nutritional needs as well as your energetic needs. For example, leafy greens can nourish the heart, while carrots and oranges nourish the sacral chakra.

226 ÷ *A practical guide to* **MAGIC IN NATURE**

Essential oils

Just as certain foods can nourish corresponding chakras, you can also balance your chakras with the essential oils of plants that hold the vibrational frequency that is in alignment with that energetic centre. You can either diffuse those oils in your space or use blends mixed in carrier oils on your pulse points.

Visualising in meditation

Meditation and visualisation techniques can influence your chakras. Visualise a ball of light in the colour corresponding to the chakra you want to balance. You can imagine that the ball is growing and engulfing you, or that you are sitting within it and being filled with its healing energy. You can also visualise the source of the light coming from the area of that chakra on your body, and getting brighter and more powerful the longer you hold that vision. Allow your intuition to guide you in your visualisation meditation. The opportunities are limited only by your imagination.

Crystal balance

Use crystals that correspond to the colours or energies of the chakra you wish to balance or align. Refer to Part 1 of this book for a full A–Z list of the crystals and their associated chakras. These crystals can be worn, held during meditation, placed on the body or grids during energy healings, or placed on your altar.

By integrating these holistic practices into your daily routine you will ensure you have harmonious energy flow, leading to balanced and aligned chakras. This improves your physical, emotional and spiritual self, and leads to a more fulfilling life. Start with small steps and gradually build up to a chakra balancing practice that works for you.

THE MAGIC IN YOU ✦ 227

MERIDIANS

Meridians are the invisible pathways in your body that carry life-force energy, also known as 'qi' (pronounced 'chee'). The philosophy and teachings of the meridians originates from traditional Chinese medicine (TCM), which has been practised for thousands of years. TCM is based on the understanding that the body is an integrated union of the physical, emotional and spiritual aspects, which are all interconnected through the flow of your qi. This system of pathways transports the energy needed to nourish your organs, tissues and cells. They are essential for maintaining harmony and balance within your body.

When your pathways are clear, you will experience health, vitality and overall well-being. When you have energetic blockages or imbalances in your meridians you may experience physical, emotional or spiritual issues.

There are 12 primary meridians, each corresponding to specific organ functions. The 12 meridians are as follows: lung, large intestine, stomach, spleen, heart, small intestine, bladder, kidney, pericardium, triple heater, gallbladder and liver. Each meridian follows its own path through your body. Like a river, each pathway connects in different parts of your body to create a larger system that allows energy to flow freely. Each of the meridians are explored below, to empower you to take charge of your health and come to understand the intricate systems of energy and magic within you.

Understanding each entry

Each meridian entry denotes the correspondences for the following: yin/yang, bodily functions, emotions, element, season, colour, timing and foods.

Yin and yang: each organ is assigned as being either 'yin' or 'yang'. In TCM philosophy, yin and yang are opposing energetic forces, such as dark and light, passive and active, cold and hot. Despite being opposite, they are dependent on each other. You can utilise their competitive nature by using them to restore balance in your body and harmony in your life. For example, if an organ is out of balance and has too much or too little yin, specific foods or treatments can be applied to restore balance. A TCM practitioner will be able to diagnose yin and yang imbalances in your body.

Yin excess/yang deficiency symptoms: fatigue, cold hands and feet, pale skin, slow metabolism, congestion, nausea, swelling, apathy and low libido.

Yang excess/yin deficiency symptoms: hyperactivity, over-heated body, red skin, inflammation, fever, insomnia, constipation, night sweats, anxiety and dry throat.

Associated physical correspondences: knowing which organs and bodily functions are influenced by each meridian helps you to identify health issues or energetic imbalances.

Corresponding emotions: emotions are linked to the meridians and can help us to understand the symbiotic relationship between our physical and emotional health. This awareness can guide us to understand our patterns, identify imbalances and address healing.

Element: each meridian is associated with an element, which can help us to understand its energetic qualities. Read more about the elements in TCM on page 234.

THE MAGIC IN YOU + 229

Season: each meridian is linked to a specific season, which influences their energy flow. By gaining understanding of the seasons corresponding to each meridian, you are able to confidently align your healing practices with the cycles of the earth and approach your life in a truly holistic way. For example, eating seasonally appropriate foods will nourish the meridian associated with that season during its peak period.

Colour: each meridian is associated with a colour, which can be applied when using colour therapy to balance energy or promote healing in an area of the body governed by that meridian. You can integrate colour therapy in a number of ways, including through visualisation, in your surroundings, with your clothing, foods and more.

Timing: the timing of the meridians refers to the meridian clock, which provides insight into the approximate peak times of the day or night that the meridian's energy is at its most active. This information can help you to plan your phases of activity, rest, meals and so on throughout the day. It can also offer insights into why you feel restless at certain times of the day or why you wake in the night at the same time recurrently.

Foods to support: your diet plays an important role in maintaining your health. Knowing which foods support the meridians helps you to choose nourishing meals to support healing when addressing specific health concerns, enhance energy flow, or nurture optimal organ function.

230 ÷ *A practical guide to* **MAGIC IN NATURE**

Lung – yin

Associated physical correspondences: respiratory system, immune system and skin

Corresponding emotions: grief, sadness, inspiration

Element: metal

Season: autumn

Colour: white

Timing: 3:00–5:00 am

Foods to support: pears, radish, almonds

Large intestine – yang

Associated physical correspondences: body waste, digestive health, detoxification

Corresponding emotions: guilt, regret, letting go

Element: metal

Season: autumn

Colour: white

Timing: 5:00–7:00 am

Foods to support: whole grains, leafy greens

Stomach – yang

Associated physical correspondences: digestion, nutrient absorption, mental clarity

Corresponding emotions: anxiety, worry, trust

Element: earth

Season: late summer

Colour: yellow

Timing: 7:00–9:00 am

Foods to support: warm foods, grains, root vegetables

Spleen – yin

Associated physical correspondences: blood production, immune system, nutrient absorption

Corresponding emotions: overthinking, grounding

Element: earth

Season: late summer

Colour: yellow

Timing: 9:00–11:00 am

Foods to support: warm cooked foods, sweet potato, squash

Heart – yin

Associated physical correspondences: blood circulation, emotional well-being, consciousness

Corresponding emotions: joy, happiness, love

Element: fire

Season: summer

Colour: red

Timing: 11:00 am–1:00 pm

Foods to support: bitter foods, dark leafy greens, bitter melon

Small intestine – yang

Associated physical correspondences: digestion, nutrient absorption, mental clarity, decision making

Corresponding emotions: clarity, discernment

Element: fire

Season: summer

Colour: red

Timing: 1:00–3:00 pm

Foods to support: light meals, easy to digest foods, green vegetables

Bladder – yang

Associated physical correspondences: urinary function, detoxification, nervous system support

Corresponding emotions: fear, insecurity

Element: water

Season: winter

Colour: blue, black

Timing: 3:00–5:00 pm

Foods to support: soup, seafood, berries

Kidney – yin

Associated physical correspondences: energy reserves, reproductive health, bone strength

Corresponding emotions: safety, willpower, vitality

Element: water

Season: winter

Colour: blue, black

Timing: 5:00–7:00 pm

Foods to support: kidney beans, black beans, sea vegetables

Pericardium – yang

Associated physical correspondences: protects heart, regulates emotions, circulation

Corresponding emotions: joy, intimacy

Element: fire

Season: summer

Colour: red

Timing: 7:00–9:00 pm

Foods to support: cooling foods, cucumber, melon, mint

Triple heater – yin

Associated physical correspondences: body temperature, fluid balance, immune system

Corresponding emotions: stress, sadness, joy

Element: fire

Season: summer
Colour: red
Timing: 9:00–11:00 pm
Foods to support: light foods, green tea

Gallbladder – yang

Associated physical correspondences: digestion, decision making, muscular health

Corresponding emotions: resentment, frustration, courage

Element: wood

Season: spring

Colour: green

Timing: 11:00 pm–1:00 am

Foods to support: sour foods, citrus, vinegar

Liver – yin

Associated physical correspondences: detoxification, emotional balance, menstrual health

Corresponding emotions: anger, annoyance, creativity

Element: wood

Season: spring

Colour: green
Timing: 1:00–3:00 am
Foods to support: leafy greens, cruciferous vegetables, dandelion

The FIVE elements of TCM

Taking time to understand the five elements in TCM allows you to self-reflect and develop a focused view of the way the elements are influencing your life. When you read the entries opposite you may feel that one of the elements is particularly relatable to you at this current time. This signifies that you are being more strongly governed by that element than any other. By recognising which elements are dominant or deficient, you can work towards balance and harmony.

Wood

Wood is associated with the qualities of growth, expansion and creativity.

Emotions: anger, benevolence, kindness.

Fire

Fire is associated with the qualities of heat, intensity and transformation.

Emotions: joy, love, enthusiasm, restlessness.

Earth

Earth is associated with the qualities of stability, nourishment and balance.

Emotions: worry, sympathy, nurturing.

Metal

Metal is associated with the qualities of purification, structure and resilience.

Emotions: grief, courage, integrity.

Water

Water is associated with the qualities of fluidity, introspection and regeneration.

Emotions: fear, calmness, wisdom.

AURAS

Your aura is the magnetic field or energetic field that surrounds your body. Every living creature has an aura, which changes and adjusts to each individual depending on their mood, what energy they are emanating and their health. You are more than a physical body; you have multiple layers of energetic bodies and a spirit connected as one, existing within multiple dimensions and influencing you on a physical, emotional, mental and spiritual level.

Auras are invisible to most, although some individuals with a strong psychic sense, or who are very energetically sensitive to their surroundings, may be able to see or sense the aura's of those around them. A person's aura appears as a light or cloud of colour around them, and may show multiple colours depending on their energy, emotional state and so on. With practice, you can learn to sense auras too. To understand the meaning of the colours seen in an aura, read the colour correspondences below.

- Red – passion, competitive, determination, strength, grounded
- Orange – excitement, confidence, leadership, energy, creativity
- Yellow – joyful, friendly, intelligent, freedom, inspiration
- Green – healing, compassionate, balance, growth
- Blue – intuition, communication, clarity, emotions
- Indigo – wisdom, spirituality, empathetic, calm, intuition
- Purple – higher consciousness, spirituality, psychic power, vision
- White – purity, truth, divine connection
- Black – blocked energy, fear, shame, guilt

THE MAGIC IN YOU ✥ 237

In embracing the magic within, you recognise your deep connection to the natural world surrounding you. This is a significant step towards harnessing the magic that exists in both nature and yourself. By aligning with the natural rhythms and cycles, expanding your knowledge of the intricate energetic systems of your body and learning to energetically cleanse and align, you are cultivating a powerful holistic foundation for well-being and balance.

Whether through the use of tools, rituals or integrated holistic practices, the path to maintaining your energy and magic are uniquely your own. Remember that you are an integral part of nature, interconnected with the universe, and that your existence alone contributes to the enchantment of the world. Embrace your magic, honour your value, trust your intuition and allow the wisdom of ancient knowledge to guide you towards a more fulfilling and mystical life.

You are magic, a testament to the miraculous nature of life in itself. Nurture your connection to the magic hidden in nature so that you may fully realise the potential of the enchantment that surrounds you.

238 ✢ *A practical guide to* **MAGIC IN NATURE**

ACKNOWLEDGEMENTS

First and foremost, I want to thank Lisa Hanrahan and Paul Dennett of Rockpool Publishing for giving me the opportunity to share my passion for the everyday magic found in nature. Thank you so much for believing in me! You have built an amazing team that reflects the kind, encouraging and inspiring culture you have created, and it's a privilege to be published by you.

To the entire Rockpool team – you work tirelessly behind the scenes, making us authors shine while rarely getting the credit you deserve. Thank you so much.

A special thank you to my designer Sara Lindberg, who captured my vision from the start and brought it to life. Thank you to my amazing editors Heather Millar and Katie Stackhouse, your attention to detail is remarkable!

This book wouldn't exist were it not for the support and sacrifice of my incredible husband, Jed. Thank you for your endless encouragement and love. Despite our busy life with twin toddlers and two businesses, you always find ways to support my dreams. You're an amazing partner and we are so blessed to have you.

To my beautiful children, who are much too young to read this yet: I hope you'll grow to love this book. You were right here on my lap as I wrote these pages. You are as much a part of this as I am.

To my parents and siblings – you are as loved as you are loud. My connection with nature started in childhood with you all, reading herbal remedies with Mum and gardening with Dad. To all my friends and family who have loved me and supported me throughout this process, thank you.

Finally a thought for all those who still face oppression for their religious or spiritual beliefs. The fight for acceptance is still ongoing, and I dedicate this to every soul bravely sharing their gifts, ceremonies and prayers with the world – thank you.

INDEX

abundance 28, 29, 34, 35, 40, 44, 51, 59, 69, 85, 87, 88, 108, 109, 117, 125, 128, 132, 135, 162, 172, 191, 218
acceptance 25, 40
action 26, 209
adaptability 164, 166, 168, 169, 172
adoration 103
adventure 169
affirmations 226
agate 12; blue lace 58, 59; fire 35, 58, 61
aggression 191
agility 169
agrimony 81
air *see* wind
ajna chakra 221
allspice 81
aloe vera 99
altar 205
amazonite 21, 60
amber 21, 58
ambition 47
amethyst 21, 29, 59, 60
amplification 32, 35
anahata chakra 222
ancestral guidance 42
angel's trumpet 100
angelica 100, 149
angelite 21, 60
angels 21, 22, 186; communication with 51; connection with 26
anger 22, 37, 233, 235
animal sacrifice 161
animals 151–79; as messengers 153–4; earth association of 178; fire association of 179; water association of 179; wind association of 178
anise 81–2
annoyance 233
anointing 81
ant 157
anxiety 58, 68, 231; *see also* stress
apatite 21, 60
aphrodisiacs 84
apophyllite 22
apple 121, 146

apricot 121, 144
aquamarine 22, 59, 60
aragonite 22
arnica 100–1, 148
aromatherapy blends 69
ashwagandha 139, 147
assertiveness 176
astragalus 101
attraction 92, 108, 172
auras 236–8; cleansing 32
auric field 15
authority 195
aventurine 22, 59, 60; red 47–8
avocado 121
awakening 25, 84
azurite 22, 59, 60

balance 25, 26, 51, 53, 55, 57, 59, 104, 139, 162, 175, 235, 237
banana 121–2
banishing 103, 115
banishing 83, 85, 87, 92, 93, 95, 97, 127, 134, 218
barley 87–8
basil 82, 147
baths 75, 216
bay laurel 82
bear 157
beauty 99, 114, 116, 124, 169, 172, 175
bee 158
beeswax candles 159
beetle 160
beetroot 122
beginnings 42, 166, 199, 201
belladonna 83
benevolence 235
betony wood 118
bird 161
birth 168
black tourmaline 23, 59
bladder 232
blessed thistle 101
blessings 100, 101, 201
blockages 38
bloodstone 24, 58
bloody dock 84
blue butterfly pea flower 101, 147
blue calcite 25, 59

blue chalcedony 58
blue lace agate 25, 58, 59, 60
blue lotus 102
blue tourmaline 25, 59
blueberry 122
body organs 17, 187
bone broth 72
bones 161, 163
boundaries 24
buffalo 162
business 176
butterfly 162, 178

cabbage 122
cacao 123
calamus root 139
calcite 25; blue 25, 59, green 36, 59; orange 44
calendula 103
calm 21, 26, 37, 47, 48, 88, 101, 104, 170, 235, 237
candles 215, 217–18; colours and 218; making of 159
cannabis 103, 149
caper 84
cardamom 84
career 218
carnation 103
carnelian 26, 58
carrier oils 69
carrot 124
castor bean plant 103–4
cat 162, 178
catmint 104
cavansite 26, 59, 60
celestial bodies 191–201; angels and gods and 185; body organs and 187; chakras and 176; colours and 185; crystals and 186; elements and 185; metals and 185; planets 183; plants and 186; stars 183; weekdays and 184; zodiac and 185; *see also* individual planets
celestine 26
celestite 26, 58
centring 37
ceremony 15
chakras 17–18, 220–4; alignment of 226; celestial bodies

240

and 187; crown 221; heart 222; root 224; sacral 223; solar plexus 223; third eye 221; throat 222
chalcedony 12, 26; blue 58
chamomile 104, 147
change 58, 160, 162, 165, 192, 201
charoite 27, 58, 60
chaste berry 104
cherry 124
chiastolite 27, 60
chicken 163
chilli pepper 85
chrysanthemum 105
chrysocolla 27
chrysoprase 28, 59, 61
cinnabar 28
cinnamon 85, 146
citrine 29, 59
clairvoyance 25
clarity 30, 32, 43, 52, 57, 84, 86, 87, 89, 90, 93, 94, 101, 106, 111, 117, 139, 169, 201, 218, 232, 237
cleansing 35, 52, 82, 88, 95, 109, 118, 175, 197, 218
clear quartz 30, 58
clearing 22
clove 86
colours 184, 218, 230; auras and 237
comfort 26, 42, 100, 170
communication 21, 22, 25, 26, 32, 37, 40, 54, 101, 165, 177, 189, 207, 218, 222, 237
community 157, 158, 177
companionship 165
compassion 33, 34, 38, 44, 48, 49, 54, 90, 222, 237
competitiveness 237
confidence 172
confidence 26, 28, 49, 54, 58, 218, 223, 237
connection 174
consciousness 32, 117
consecration 140
contracts 176
cooling 197
corn 124
cornflower 104
cosmic expansion 41
courage 24, 33, 44, 48, 49, 54, 57, 58, 84, 91, 92, 96, 114, 117, 127, 157, 166, 169, 170, 191, 218, 233, 235
coyote 164

cranberry 125, 148
creativity 26, 27, 28, 35, 40, 48, 57, 172, 174, 189, 218, 233, 235, 237
cross-references 5
crow 164
crown chakra *see* sahasrara chakra
crystals A–Z of 21–63; as jewellery 15; as magical tools 11; balancing of 227; body organs and 17; burying of 14; care of 12–14; celestial bodies and 186; ceremony and 15; chakras and 17–18; combinations of 58–9; dusting of 12; elements and 18; energy of 13; flowers and 14; grids and 16, 216; healing energies of 11; home use 16; meditation and 16; meridians and 17; Mohs hardness of 18; moonlight and 13; oils and 14; profiles of 17–18; properties of 18; salt and 14; smoke cleansing of 13; sound and 14; sun exposure and 12; use of 15–16; water cleaning of 12, 14; wearing of 15; *see also* individual crystals
cucumber 125, 148
cumin 85
cunning 164, 168
cuprite 32
curiosity 162, 172
curses 85

daffodil 105
Dalmatian jasper 32, 61
danburite 32, 61
dandelion 106
death 164
decision making 30, 35
deer 164–5, 178
defence 89
defensive magic 97
desert rose 32
desire 121, 137
determination 26, 48, 54, 174, 237
detoxification 24
devil's claw 125
devil's snare 87
diamond 32
diet 2326
dill 87

diopside 33
dioptase 33, 61
discernment 168, 170, 232
discipline 157, 192
divination 100
divine connection 35, 41, 53, 108, 200, 218, 237
divine feminine 42, 174
divine guidance 33, 165
dog 165, 178
dolphin 165, 179
dominance 170, 175
domination 174
dove 165
dragon 165–6
dragonfly 166
dragon's blood jasper 33
dragon's blood resin 139–40
dreams 38, 192
dreamwork 113, 115
dumortierite 33, 61

eagle 166, 178
earth (element) 205, 206; association of with animals 178; connection with 36, 51; medicine of 42; *see also* elements
Earth (planet) 190
echinacea 107, 148
eggs 161
Egyptian glass *see* Libyan desert glass
elderflower 107
electromagnetic protection 51
elements 18, 203–9; celestial bodies and 185; meridians and 229; working with 206; *see also* earth; fire; water; wind
elephant 167
elk 168
emerald 34
emotions 21, 25, 36, 89, 177, 201, 208, 218, 237; awareness of 47; balancing of 57, 197; big 59; expression of 223; growth of 44; healing of 33, 36, 37, 49, 47, 57, 94; meridians and 229
empathy 222, 237
empowerment 29, 44, 49
endurance 32, 139, 140, 169
energy 237; amplification of 49; blockages in 50, 237; clearing of 215–16; comforting 26; divine light

INDEX ÷ 241

22, 50; energy elements and 205; goddess 42; life-force 32, 38; transmutation of 30; trickster 164
enthusiasm 235
epidote 34, 61
essential oils 68–9, 227
eucalyptus 87
evil eye 81, 86
evil spirits 175
excitement 237
expansion 33, 37, 191, 235
expression 21, 25, 26, 38, 39, 55, 222

faith 168
family 167, 170, 218
fear 26, 47, 232, 235, 237
fearlessness 21, 22
feathers 161
feminine 77–8, 171
fennel 127
fertility 69, 73, 88, 91, 92, 104, 111, 115, 121, 122, 124, 125, 126, 128, 135, 136, 143, 144, 158, 163, 168, 172, 174, 218
feverfew 107
fidelity 85, 130
fig 126, 205
fire 209, 235; association of with animals 179; see also elements
fire agate 35, 58, 61
flowers 98–119; growing of 67; see also individual flowers
fluidity 235
fluorite 35, 59, 61
focus 2, 33, 35, 53, 69, 89, 169
food 230
forgiveness 33, 49
fortune 165
fox 168, 179
foxglove 107–8
frankincense resin 140
freedom 16, 161, 169, 237
fresh starts 166
friendliness 237
friendship 165, 218
frog 168, 179
fruits 120–37; see also individual fruits
frustration 233
fuchsite 35; ruby 49, 63
fulgurite 35, 61

gallbladder 233

garlic 127, 148
garnet 36, 58, 61
gentleness 47, 164, 167, 172
ginger 127
ginseng root 140
glamour 172
glass 43
goals 36
gods 186
goethite 36
golden tektite see Libyan desert glass
grace 162, 171, 172, 175
grains 87–8
grape 128, 144
grapefruit 128
grasshopper 168, 178
gratitude 162, 200
green calcite 36, 59
green tourmaline 36
grids 15, 216
grief 231, 235
grounding 22, 23, 27, 32, 33, 35, 36, 37, 40, 42, 43, 47, 51, 52, 53, 55, 56, 85, 88, 95, 96, 134, 206, 215–16, 218, 224, 231, 237
growth 35, 57, 162, 164, 177, 191, 235, 237
guidance 165, 169, 176
guilt 231, 237

habits 56, 200
happiness 28, 29, 46, 89, 91, 93, 103, 104, 128, 218, 231
harmony 25, 32, 38, 40, 51, 53, 57, 165, 189, 218
hawk 169
healing 24, 38, 40, 41, 57, 58, 69, 73, 81, 82, 86, 87, 88, 90, 91, 92, 94, 97, 99, 100, 101, 103, 105, 107, 112, 114, 115, 116, 117, 118, 121, 125, 130, 131, 134, 135, 136, 137, 139, 140, 157, 169, 174, 195, 218, 237
health 108, 109, 112, 119, 121, 122, 126, 127, 129, 137, 148, 197, 206, 218
heart 231; alignment of 38, 54; expansion of 22, 36, 45, 56, 122; healing of 35, 36, 41
heart chakra see anahata chakra
heat 235
heather 108
hematite 36–7, 58, 61

hemimorphite 37
herbs 80–97; baths 74–5; drying of 70; gardens 67; spells and 70; tincture 68
hexes 81, 87, 92, 93, 97, 119, 122, 175
hibiscus 108
higher consciousness 221, 237
higher knowing 161
home 218
honesty 108
honeysuckle 108–9
hope 44, 47, 165
horse 169
house plants 73–4
howlite 37, 58, 61
hummingbird 169, 178
humour 164
hyssop 109

imagination 49, 192, 207
immunity 101
improvement 199
independence 162, 177
indicolite 25
indigo gabbro 37
individualism 192
indulgence 189
influence 84, 130
inner truth 39
innocence 162, 164, 175
innovation 192
insecurity 232
insight 169, 170, 171
inspiration 100, 231, 237
instability 201
instinct 174, 177
integrity 172, 235
intellect/ intelligence 164, 172, 189, 207, 218, 237
intensity 235
intentions 199, 200, 201
intestine: large 231; small 232
intimacy 232
introspection 37, 49, 157, 235
intuition 5, 22, 25, 26, 27, 33, 37, 38, 49, 53, 54, 102, 111, 135, 162, 164, 169, 171, 192, 197, 208, 218, 221, 237
iolite 37–8, 58, 62

jade 38, 58, 62
jaguar 169
jasmine 109, 149
jasper: Dalmatian 32, 61; dragon's blood 33; ocean 44; red 48

242 ✦ *A practical guide to* MAGIC IN NATURE

jewellery 15; botanical 70–1;
  rose petal beads 71
joy 28, 37, 40, 44, 58, 69, 84,
  91, 94, 111, 115, 124, 132,
  164, 165, 169, 218, 223,
  231, 232, 235, 237
juniper 88, 145
Jupiter 191

kangaroo 169
karmic cycles 42
kidney 232
kindness 48, 235
kitchen witch 72–3
knowledge 51
koala 170
kunzite 38, 59, 62
kyanite 38, 62

labradorite 38, 62
lapis lazuli 39
larimar 40, 59
lavender 110
leadership 44, 49, 170, 174,
  237
lemon 128
lemon balm 88
lemongrass 88
lepidolite 40, 58, 62
letting go 231
Libyan desert glass 40, 59, 62
licorice 130, 146
life-force energy 38
life path 40, 41
lily 111, 144
lily of the valley 111, 145
lime 130
limitation 192
lion 170, 179
liver 233
lodestone 40–1
longevity 176
lotus: blue 102; sacred 117
love 34, 38, 45, 47, 48, 49, 54,
  57, 59, 69, 73, 75, 81, 82,
  84, 85, 87, 88, 89, 90, 92,
  93, 97, 101, 103, 104, 105,
  107, 108, 109, 114, 116,
  117, 118, 121, 122, 123,
  124, 130, 134, 135, 137,
  146, 165, 175, 189, 222,
  231, 235
loyalty 165, 177
luck 59, 81, 84, 87, 91, 96, 97,
  105, 108, 122, 134, 137,
  167, 168, 174, 201, 218
luna moth 170

lung 231

magic 164, 165, 173, 176, 201
magic: defensive 97; in nature
  205; personal 211–18
magnetic field 236–8
magnetite see lodestone
majesty 167
malachite 41, 59
mandrake root 143
manifesting 28, 33, 35, 36, 40,
  49, 53, 75, 174, 201
manipura chakra 223
mantis 170
marigold 111–12
marjoram 88
Mars 191
marshmallow 90
masculine 77–8
materialism 206
meditation 21, 22, 32, 59, 109,
  170, 215, 218, 227; crystals
  and 16; experiences of 21
memory 48, 93, 218
mercury 28
Mercury 189
meridians 17, 228–35
metal 185, 235
metamorphosis 168
meteorite 41, 58
milk thistle 112
mind 207
mindfulness 170
mint 90
modesty 171
Mohs hardness 18
moisturising 99, 197
moldavite 41, 58
money 59, 218
mookaite 42
moon 196–7; bath 75; black
  201; blood 201; blue 201;
  connection with 170; phases
  of 199–201; super 201;
  super blood 201
moonstone 42, 58
morganite 42, 59, 62
moth 170, 178
motherwort 112, 147
mouse 171, 178
mugwort 113
muladhara chakra 224
mulberry 130
mullein 114
myrrh resin 140
mystery 162, 169
mystic merlinite see indigo

gabbro

nature 205, 213; connection
  with 35, 47
negativity 218
Neptune 192
nettle 117
nourishment 197, 235
nurturing 49, 170, 235
nurturing 49
nutmeg 90–1

oats 87–8
observation 200
obsidian 43, 59; rainbow 47;
  snowflake 53
obstacles 172
ocean jasper 44
offering 96
oils: carrier 69; essential 68–9,
  227
olive 131
onion 133
opal 44, 58, 62
open heartedness 48
opportunities 46, 168
optimism 22, 29
orange 132
orange calcite 44
orchid 114
oregano 91
organs 187
overthinking 231
overwhelm 201
owl 171

palo santo 141
panther 171, 179
paprika 91
parsley 91–2
partnership 175
passion 35, 47, 49, 85, 91, 121,
  124, 218, 237
past-life recall 21, 27, 38
patience 22, 170, 174
pea flower 101, 147
peace 26, 45, 51, 97, 104, 110,
  112, 118, 131, 161, 165,
  170, 218
peach 133
peacock 172, 179
pear 133–4
pearl 45
pendulums 217
peony 115
pepper 92
pericardium 232

INDEX ÷ 243

peridot 46, 58
perseverance 33, 41
persimmon 134
physical healing 41
physicality 206
pineapple 134
pink tourmaline 47, 58, 62
planets 183
planning 176
plants 65–149; celestial bodies and 76, 186; chakras and 79; characteristics of 78; elements and 77; energy profiles of 77–8; fertility and 144; flowers and shrubs 98–119; fruit and vegetables 120–37; health and well-being and 148; herbs and spices 80–97; introduction to 67–75; love and 146; magical power of 79; moon and 197; names of 76; planting of 67–8; poisonous 83, 100, 104, 111; profiles of 76–9; protection and 145; roots, resins and woods 138–43; spiritual connection and 149; stress relief and 147; weekdays and 76–7
platypus 172
playfulness 32, 165, 168, 172
pleasure 28, 123, 223
Pluto 193
poisonous plants 100, 104, 111
pomegranate 135
poppy 115
positivity 36, 117
potato 134
potency 84
potential 44
power 81, 82, 84, 139, 143, 157, 165, 166, 169, 170, 171, 174, 175, 195
prehnite 47, 62
pride 166
productivity 158, 176
prophecy 39, 164, 173
prosperity 22, 34, 40, 85, 90, 96, 100, 101, 103, 104, 107, 108, 109, 111, 112, 103, 121, 127, 128, 134, 135, 142, 163, 168, 218
protection 23, 27, 32, 33, 37, 38, 39, 43, 47, 51, 53, 55, 57, 59, 69, 73, 75, 81, 82, 83, 85, 87, 88, 89, 91, 92, 93, 94, 95, 96, 99, 113, 114,

115, 117, 118, 119, 122, 125, 127, 128, 129, 130, 131, 134, 135, 137, 139, 140, 141, 142, 143, 144, 160, 163, 165, 169, 171, 174, 175, 176, 191, 192, 218
psyche 193
psychic ability 21, 22, 89
psychic enhancement 51, 59, 93, 197
psychic expansion 25
psychic power 37, 53, 54, 69, 75, 83, 87, 88, 90, 96, 97, 104, 105, 106, 107, 109, 113, 218, 221, 237
psychic shield 42
Ptolemy, Claudius 187
pumpkin 136
purification 47, 51, 53, 86, 87, 88, 90, 91, 93, 94, 95, 96, 101, 107, 112, 118, 125, 129, 130, 132, 139, 140, 141, 142, 175, 197, 218, 235
purity 32, 45, 111, 114, 117, 165, 176, 237
purpose 40
pyrite 47, 59, 62

qi 228
quartz 12, 29, 59; clear 30, 58; rose 48–9, 59, 63; shapes of 31; smoky 52, 58

rabbit 172, 178
rainbow obsidian 47
raspberry 137
raspberry leaf 92–3, 144
rat 172
raven 172
rebirth 41, 105, 162, 168, 171, 173, 174, 201
recharging 201
red aventurine 47–8
red jasper 48
red raspberry leaf 92–3
reflection 176
regeneration 160, 235
regret 231
relationships 42, 85
relaxation 36, 103
release 25, 33, 38, 53, 54, 200
relief 48
renewal 36, 111, 160, 172, 174
resentment 233
resilience 24, 84, 121, 235
resins 138–43
resourcefulness 163, 171

responsibility 170
rest 200
restlessness 235
rhodochrosite 48, 59, 63
rhodonite 48
rice 87–8
ritual bath 216
romance 218
root chakra *see* muladhara chakra
roots 138–43
rose 116; petal beads 71
rose quartz 48–9, 59, 63
rosemary 93, 145
ruby 49, 58
ruby fuchsite 49, 63
rue 93, 145
rutile 49, 58, 59, 63

sacral chakra *see* svadhisthana chakra
sacred lotus 117 177
sadness 231, 232
safety 232
saffron 93–4
sage 94
sahasrara chakra 221
salt 95
sandalwood 142
sapphire 49, 63
Saturn 192
seasons 230
security 36, 218, 224
selenite 14, 50, 59
self-acceptance 47
self-awareness 27
self-care 22, 42
self-expression 49
self-guidance 32
self-love 35, 42, 48, 49
self-worth 47
sensitivity 45, 164, 172
sensuality 174
septarian 51
seraphinite 51, 63
serenity 25, 40, 45
serpent 174
serpentine 51, 63
sexual freedom 223
sexuality 57
shadow work 43
shame 237
shark 174, 179
shielding 23
shrubs 98–119; *see also* individual shrubs
shungite 51, 58, 59

244 ✢ *A practical guide to* **MAGIC IN NATURE**

skill 171
sleep 40, 69, 81, 104, 110, 115; aid for 32; improvement of 37
smoke cleansing 215
smoky quartz 52, 58
snake 178
sneezeweed 118
snowflake obsidian 53
sodalite 53, 63
solar plexus chakra *see* manipura chakra
solitude 157
soothing 22, 99, 197
speed 169
spells 70
spices 80–97
spider 174, 179
spirit 169; communication with 32, 96, 100
spiritual: awareness 221; connection 32, 123, 170, 221; development 218; evolution 51; expansion 41, 53, 103; growth 27, 177; guidance 169; messenger 171; self 201
spirituality 33, 37, 54, 57, 69, 100, 102, 140, 141, 142, 161, 192, 237
spleen 231
St John's wort 94
stability 37, 47, 51, 56, 57, 122, 176, 206, 218, 235
stag 174–5
stamina 168
star anise 96
stars 183
staurolite 53
stealth 168, 169
stillness 37, 170, 200
stinging nettle 117
stomach 231
strawberry 137, 146
strength 22, 32, 33, 37, 41, 47, 91, 101, 107, 111, 117, 118, 125, 127, 134, 139, 140, 157, 162, 166, 167, 168, 169, 170, 171, 174, 175, 218, 237
stress 35, 40, 46, 47, 52, 58, 69, 232; *see also* anxiety
structure 235
subconscious 173, 208
substitutions 5
success 90, 195, 199
sugilite 53–4, 63

sun 194–5
sunflower 117
sunstone 54, 58
survival 162, 168, 172, 174
svadhisthana chakra 223
swan 175, 179
sweetness 158
sympathy 235

tangibility 206
tanzanite 54, 59, 63
tea 68
teamwork 157, 177
tektite 40
third eye chakra *see* ajna chakra
thistle: blessed 101; milk 112
throat chakra *see* vishuddha chakra
thyme 96
tiger 175, 179
tiger eye 54, 58, 63
timing 230
toad 175–6
tobacco 96–7, 149
tomato 137
tools 217
tourmaline: black 23, 59; blue 25, 59, 60; green 36; pink 47, 58, 62; watermelon 57, 63
traditional Chinese medicine 228, 234–5
tranquillity 21, 24, 50, 88, 102
transformation 21, 27, 28, 33, 35, 36, 37, 38, 41, 49, 51, 53, 57, 130, 158, 160, 162, 166, 170, 173, 174, 175, 192, 201, 209, 235
trickery 168
trickster energy 164
triple heater 232–3
trust 22, 231
truth 26, 27, 39, 166, 222, 237
turmeric root 142
turquoise 55, 58
turtle 176

unakite 56
underestimation 171
unicorn 176
unity 41, 162
Uranus 192

vanadinite 57
vegetables 67–8, 120–37; *see also* individual vegetables
Venus 189

vervain 117–8
vibrational energy 23
violet 118
violet leaf 97
Virginia sneezeweed 118
vishuddha chakra 222
vision 237
visions 37, 83, 87, 100, 102
visualisation 215, 227
vitality 35, 36, 41, 47, 51, 57, 84, 91, 101, 118, 124, 128, 139, 140, 218, 232

wasp 176–7
water 205, 208, 235; association of with animals 179; cleaning of crystals with 12; *see also* elements
watermelon tourmaline 57, 63
wattle 118
wealth 28, 81, 82, 86, 87, 91, 93, 123, 126, 135, 139
weekdays 184
well-being 38, 148
wellness 73, 110
whale 177
wheat 87–8
will 47
willpower 44, 51, 54, 232
wind 161, 205, 207; association of with animals 178; *see also* elements
wisdom 27, 40, 53, 94, 130, 167, 171, 173, 174, 177, 218, 235, 237
wishbone ritual 163
wishes 106
wolf 177
wolfsbane 97
wonder 44, 176
wood betony 118
woods 138–43, 235
worry 231, 235

yang 229
yarrow
yin 229
yoga 226
youthfulness 122, 165

zircon 57
zodiac signs 185
zoisite 57

INDEX + 245

ABOUT THE AUTHOR

Jessica Lahoud is an author, artist and co-owner of Australia's iconic crystal store, Mineralism. With a deep fascination for the magic hidden in nature and the interconnectedness of all living beings, Jessica's writing invites her readers to explore the enchantment surrounding them and uncover the profound reflections of humanity mirrored in the natural world.

As a third-generation gem merchant, Jessica's upbringing immersed her in the world of crystals, where she developed an intuitive understanding of the subtle energies and healing properties of crystals, plants and all natural things. She spends her days offering these insights to Australia's spiritual community and continues to travel the world to source crystals for Mineralism.

Jessica is also the author of *Crystal Companions: An A–Z Guide* and *Crystal Flashcards*.

mineralism.com.au | ⓘ mineralism_aus